THE BRAZILIAN COOKBOOK

THE
BRAZiLiaN
COOKBOOK

BY IRENE BECKER MOLITERNO

Translated and Adapted by
CHARLES FRANK & ASSOCIATES

 CHARLES FRANK PUBLICATIONS, INC. ● NEW YORK 36, N.Y.

Table of Contents

$\mathcal{F}$IFTY or so years ago, Henry Van Dyke, in a philosophical moment, wrote some words still very applicable today:

"Individuality is the salt of common life. You may have to live in a crowd, but you do not have to live like it, nor subsist on its food."

Which brings us to the heart of the matter —and of this book.

Too many of us live like the crowd, subsisting on its food —and missing some of the salt in life (at least, when it comes to eating). We fall into the easy but unimaginative rhythm of serving steak, French fries and peas for dinner or roast beef, mashed potatoes and string beans for supper. If the day —and the children— have been particularly wearing, canned tuna fish casserole is a third, simple solution to the what-shall-we-eat problem.

True. Hubby likes steak and potatoes; the children are wild about tuna fish casserole. Someone we once knew had a lettuce and Swiss cheese sandwich on white bread as steady lunchtime fare for at least 17 consecutive years.

He would have liked other food, too, but he never realized what he was missing. Where eating is concerned, few people do. Like the proverbially contented cow, they're content to keep on re-chewing the same old cud.

It's a pity because it doesn't take much more imagination —and certainly, very little additional effort— to transform common food into outstanding meals. With *The Brazilian Cookbook,* it doesn't take any imagination at all.

The Brazilians —unhampered by all the leisure and diversions most Americans have at their disposal— of necessity have learned to make every opportunity for enjoyment count. That's why they don't simply *subsist* on food —they *dine* on it. Once you've tried some of their favorite dishes (you'll find the recipes for them in this cookbook) you'll understand the difference. You'll see why in Brazil every meal, no matter how simple, is a feast.

Brazilian cuisine, you see, is quite different from the usual American or "continental" cuisine served in most of our homes and restaurants —but it is not so exotic that it need frighten the less-than-adventuresome eater. Even the die-hard steak and potatoes addict will enjoy the change.

Most of the ingredients in a Brazilian recipe are ingredients familiar to American supermarket shelves. It's the varied —and loving— way in which the Brazilians use these same old ingredients that makes the difference. In fact, the chief reason for Brazil's "gastronomic" success

8

is the large variety of dishes ordinarily served in most Brazilian homes. And chief reason for this great variety is the kaleidoscope of races which have blended to make the Brazilian people (some 80 million strong) —and Brazilian cooking— what it is today.

Originally, as was the United States, Brazil was solely populated by several primitive Indian tribes. Then in the first half of the 16th century, to this vast tropical wilderness, came the first foreign intruders: the great navigators of those days, the Portuguese. The Portuguese brought with them cattle and seed, their customs and cuisine —and the determination to stay. Stay they did.

For almost 300 years —from 1531, when Brazil was first settled by the Portuguese, until 1822, when Dom Pedro I, son of the Portuguese emperor Dom João VI, declared Brazilian independence from the mother country, Brazil was under Portuguese rule. But, though the Brazilians emancipated themselves politically from Portugal on September 7th, 1822, they couldn't rid themselves quite so easily of the old traditional ties. Brazilian cooking, thus, even today, is strongly influenced by the Portuguese cuisine of the Old World —adapted to meet the necessities of the new environment.

Yet, Brazilian cooking doesn't stop there. The Portuguese were good settlers and hard workers but, like the other Europeans, they were unaccustomed to the heavy, humid heat of the tropics. And so —as was also occurring in the other new colonies of the Western Hemisphere— African slaves were imported to work in the hot, but lucrative, sugar cane fields. The African slaves brought with them, too, their own customs, their voodoo —and *their* native recipes. Eventually, these slaves intermarried with the Brazilian Indians and the Portuguese colonizers —and left their mark on the Brazilian population and Brazilian cooking. The delicious recipes for vatapá, carurú, acarajé and cuscuz are some notable examples —and all are to be found in this cookbook.

Brazilian cooking, consequently, is probably mainly an Afro-Luso-Brazilian blend. But other cultures have had their influence, too —if only to add a soupçon to the Brazilian broth. First came the French and then later the Dutch in the guise of invadors. Though the Portuguese-Brazilians eventually succeeded in turning them back, they, too, left their traces —street names, architecture, blond and blue-eyed descendents and some typically French and Dutch dishes attest to the stay of these interlopers in certain regions of Brazil.

Next came the great waves of immigration to Brazil: Italians, Germans, Poles, Syrians, Lebanese, Japanese — all added their part to the Brazilian pot. As in the States, the cultural influence of these immigrants can be felt most strongly in the large cosmopolitan cities —such as São Paulo and Rio de Janeiro— where they flocked to by the thousands; or, in certain regional areas —such as, for example, Santa Catarina with its large German colony— where they settled.

In the large cities of Brazil, consequently, you will find that the food has a decided international flavor. On the other hand, in certain regions you may find yourself eating *heete bliksem* (Dutch pork chops with apples) or *sauerbraten* (German marinated beef) though the cook speaks Portuguese like a native —and, in fact, *is* a native or, at least, native-born.

So much for the effects of the different racial influences on Brazilian cooking. Two other factors have had an inescapable effect on national gustatory pleasures: namely, geography and climate.

Brazil has a 5,000 mile coastline pounded by the Atlantic Ocean. It has a network of 28,000 miles of waterways —including the mighty Amazon river which, when it enters Brazil, is only a mile in width but by the time it reaches the Atlantic has opened up to 180 miles wide and has such tremendous force that its fresh water shoots 150 miles out to sea. So much water, both fresh and salt, leads almost inescapably to an abundance and variety of fish and seafood. It is only natural that Brazilians, especially those living around the coastal regions and on the borders of the king of rivers —which means a large majority— are great fish and seafood (particularly shrimp) fanciers. Consequently, any really authentic Brazilian recipe book —such as *The Brazilian Cookbook*— has to devote a large portion of its pages to these favorite dishes.

Then, in the southern regions of Brazil stretch the

vast and lonely *pampas,* the rich grazing lands where the *gaúchos* (Brazilian cowboys) tend the large herds of the *estancias* (cattle ranches) which supply the Brazilian population with its wonderful beef. These happy nomads of the *pampas* carry their "kitchens" in their pack and get their food "on the hoof" since they subsist mostly on the beef from the steer they tend. From the *gaúchos* come the simple but delicious recipes for *churrasco* (meat barbecued or broiled over live coals) which have made this word almost synonymous with southern Brazil —and particularly the state of Rio Grande do Sul.

And, of course, there are the three dishes which —in one form or another— never fail to make their appearance at the Brazilian board: *feijão, arroz* and *farofa.*

Feijão is the Brazilian word for beans. Black beans, brown beans, red beans, white beans, navy beans: you name it; the Brazilians have it. Brazil, in short, is the world's major bean producer so, understandably, beans are a constant dinner companion. This may sound unpleasantly like army fare, but nothing could be further from the truth. The Brazilians prepare beans in so many delicious ways that it's no wonder they won't let a meal go by without them. In fact, the dish which —perhaps more than any other— has made Brazilian cooking internationally known is *feijoada,* a gourmet's delight consisting of black beans, sausages and an incredible variety of meats and condiments. This rich dish *must* be served with *arroz* and *farofa.*

Arroz is rice and is to most Latins what potatoes are to Americans, i.e., indispensable. In Brazil, it isn't surprising to find it served in three different ways at the same meal: in the soup, served with beans and meat and, finally, for dessert! (You'll find recipes for all three ways in this cookbook.)

Farofa is uniquely Brazilian. It is a dish made with the flour ground from the root of the manioc* or mandioc plant —of which Brazil is also the world's major producer. The Brazilians simply toast the manioc flour lightly in butter, add salt to taste and, presto!, they have a dish fit for a king. Or they may sauté minced onions, sausages, what-have-you in butter before adding the manioc flour. Or they may not bother at all and just sprinkle the *farinha* (manioc flour) as is or slightly heated on top of whatever they're eating. Whichever way it is prepared, *farofa* invariably winds up on the plate mixed in with whatever else is served for dinner that day. It is one of those truly "democratic" dishes: no matter how humble the hovel or how poor the peasant, there is always at least a tiny plot devoted to growing the manioc plant, while in the rarified stratosphere of the upper social scale, farofa is found "flourishing" on even the most elegant banquet tables. (Incidentally, most Portuguese-American groceries carry it, but if

---

* The manioc plant also goes under the names of yuca, cassava, manihot, etc.

manioc flour isn't easily available in your neighborhood, the ordinary farina you find on your supermarket shelves will substitute nicely.)

Another dish found quite often at the Brazilian dinner table is corn: fresh corn, dried corn, white corn, yellow corn or ground corn meal, in one way or another. Surprisingly enough, Brazil is NOT the world's largest corn producer —the United States is. Brazil comes in second place: 7 million tons annually compared to the States' 80 million. Nonetheless, the Brazilians outshine the Americans in the different ways they prepare (and consume) corn. Probably, the reason for this is that, here again, even the humblest *caipira* (a Brazilian "hillbilly") has a small patch devoted to growing corn for home consumption.

Then, of course, there is coffee, a commodity which Brazilians can't do without at breakfast, lunch, dinner and between-meals time. The sun, the soil, the rainfall, yes, even the gods smiled on Brazil to make it the natural habitat of the coffee plant —and the world's uncontested leader in coffee production and exportation. Considering the quantities of *cafézinhos* (demi-tasse coffee) the Brazilians consume at every hour of the day, the wonder is that they have any left to export.

Besides these staple foods, Brazil is also blessed with an almost endless variety of fruits and vegetables, but unfortunately, a good many of these are completely unknown in the United States. To cite one small example, there are some ten different kinds of bananas alone, each with its own distinctive flavor. Naturally, recipes which include these completely native foods have to be omitted from a cookbook such as this one which has been specially adapted for use outside Brazil.

These, then, are the factors which have influenced —and continue to influence— Brazilian cooking and, in consequence, have dictated the general outline of *The Brazilian Cookbook*. The recipes, nonetheless, to be included in this cookbook had to meet certain other criteria: they had to be...

... traditional *and* delicious;

... simple enough for even an unexperienced cook to prepare;

... made with ingredients which were either easily available in local markets or which could be substituted for by common ingredients without appreciably changing the flavor of the dish.

The recipes, furthermore, were specially adapted by...

... listing the ingredients separately from the instructions to shorten preparation time;

... converting Brazilian measurements to standard American measurements;

... simplifying the cooking method wherever feasible.

For convenience, the cookbook has been divided into sections separating the different dinner courses —from appetizer to coffee. In this way, you can "take the plunge" immediately by planning a completely Brazilian dinner from start to finish; or you can put your toe in first and test the water by trying out just one course at a time.

For convenience, too, there is a "Glossary for Cooks" to explain the Brazilian names used in the text, and an index to help you find any particular dish you may have in mind. In short, we've done everything possible to make *The Brazilian Cookbook* a cookbook for those who like to cook as well as for those who think cooking is a chore. Nonetheless, we humbly admit we deserve no laurels. *The Brazilian Cookbook* is just by nature a cookbook for those who like to dine —and who doesn't? Its success belongs squarely on the shoulders of the Brazilian cooks.

THE EDITORS

February 20th, 1963

APPETIZERS
and HORS D'OEUVRES

"Appetite," said Rabelais, "comes with the eating."

We can't say Rabelais was thinking specifically of the delicious appetizers served at Brazilian festas and cocktail parties because Brazil had only just been discovered at the time. But, when you taste the following recipes, you'll agree he was certainly being prophetic. And, no wonder.

Brazilians lavish almost more time and care in the preparation of appetizers and hors d'oeuvres than they do on an entire meal —possibly because there's generally a long time lapse between the usual "apéritif hour" and dinner time which is about 9 p.m. The appetizers and hors d'oeuvres, consequently, have to be good.

In any case, at any festa or "get together," you will find these tasty morsels dressed up, decorated and beautifully arranged on buffets or brought out hot and enticing straight from the kitchen. Either way, they're impossible to resist, and you will discover that "appetite does come with the eating."

SECTION ONE

········· APPETIZERS and HORS d'OEUVRES ·········

"CARIOCA" HORS D'OEUVRES

½ pound flour
¼ pound butter
¼ pound bland cheese
¼ pound grated Parmesan cheese
1 tablespoon salt

COMBINE all ingredients, mix well and form into little balls. Brush with egg yolk mixed with melted butter. Bake in a greased baking pan in a hot oven. For lighter texture, use a little less flour.

CHEESE "EMPADA"*

3 cups flour
1 egg
2 tablespoons butter
1 tablespoon baking powder
1 teaspoon salt
1 cup milk

---

* "Empada" is a tiny pie or tartlet, baked in a muffin tin or similar baking form which has been lined with pie dough and filled with meat, chicken, shrimp, hearts of palm, cheese filling, etc. —in short, filled with anything that would make a tasty morsel.

COMBINE the ingredients and mix well. Roll out and line muffin tins. Pour into each form, 1 tablespoon of cheese filling below and bake in a hot oven. These "tartlets' are baked open without a dough covering.

Cheese Filling

⅔ *pounds bland cheese*
4 *egg yolks and 4 egg whites, beaten until stiff*
1 *tablespoon butter*
½ *cup milk*

MIX ALL ingredients thoroughly and use to fill the "empada" shells.

CHICKEN "EMPADA"*

7 *heaping tablespoons of flour*
½ *tablespoon salt*
1 *tablespoon butter*
1 *tablespoon lard*
2 *egg yolks*

PLACE the flour, butter, lard, egg yolks and salt in a bowl. Knead lightly with finger tips. Form into round ball and let stand for 1 hour. If the dough becomes too dry, soften with a little butter. Break the dough into small pieces which will line the "empada" forms or muffin tins and which will be filled later. The forms are not to be

---

* See "Glossary for Cooks" on page 247.

20

greased. After filling with the chicken filling recipe given below, cover with a little of the dough and flute the pie edges. Brush with egg yolk mixed with a little butter. (The "empada" may be filled with any other filling desired.)

Chicken Filling

½ chicken
1 tablespoon lard
1 small onion
1 clove garlic pressed in salt
*   hot peppers and black pepper, to taste*
1 scallion and parsley sprig, chopped
3 tomatoes, peeled and without seeds

HEAT the lard and when hot, add the onion and tomatoes chopped together with pressed garlic and salt. Sauté lightly and add the chicken in parts, the parsley, scallion and water, little by little. Simmer until the chicken is well cooked. When the chicken is ready, remove from flame, strain the liquid and set aside. Remove the bones from the chicken, shred the meat and add to the liquid. Heat again, letting the liquid evaporate. Thicken the sauce with flour mixed in a little milk. Stir constantly to avoid lumping. Simmer until the sauce is thick and of a smooth consistency. Cool and then use as filling for the chicken "empada."

GROUND CHICKEN DRUM STICKS

1 frying chicken
1 tablespoon butter
¾ pound tomatoes
1 cup milk
5 eggs
flour (as needed)
1 pound bread crumbs
onion
garlic pressed with salt
scallion and parsley sprig
black pepper and hot peppers to taste
lard

CUT the chicken in parts and brown in a little lard or oil with the onion and garlic. When golden brown, add a little water from time to time so that the chicken simmers until cooked. Remove the bones and put meat through grinder using a fine-tooth blade. Heat 1 tablespoon butter and sauté the condiments. Add in the meat and simmer a few minutes. Thicken with 2 eggs yolks and the flour mixed in the milk. Use enough flour to give the mixture consistency. Then add the scallion chopped fine. Let cool. Form into drumstick-shaped croquettes (inserting pieces of chicken bone to act as the drumsticks with which to hold the croquettes). Dip in the bread crumbs, then lightly beaten eggs and again in the bread crumbs. Fry in lard or oil.

COLD CUTS "CAKE"

1 *pound assorted cold cuts*
2 *pounds potatoes*
4 *cups mayonnaise, according to taste*
  chopped parsley

BOIL the potatoes and mash while hot. Grind or mince the cold cuts. Combine the potatoes, cold cuts, parsley and 2 cups mayonnaise. Arrange in plate like a cake. Cover with the rest of the mayonnaise and garnish as desired. Serve chilled.

LITTLE HAM DELIGHTS

5 *egg whites*
½ *pound grated Parmesan cheese*
1 *tablespoon flour*
½ *pound ham, ground*
  salt and black pepper to taste
2 *or 3 eggs for breading*
  bread crumbs
  oil or lard for frying

BEAT the egg whites until stiff, adding a teaspoonful of cold water. Immediately add the cheese, the ground ham, black pepper and flour. Mix well and form into little oblong balls. Dip twice alternately into lightly beaten eggs and bread crumbs. Fry in hot lard or oil until golden brown. Serve immediately.

HORS D'OEUVRES "LUCENA"

½ *pound ham*
½ *pound salami*
½ *pound Italian sausage*
⅛ *pound dill pickles*
1 *tablespoon butter*
1 *tablespoon Worcestershire sauce*
2 *tablespoons flour*
1 *tablespoon ketchup*

COMBINE the ham, sausage, salami and pickles in meat grinder. To the mixture add the butter, Worcestershire sauce, flour and ketchup. Mix well and place in pot over medium flame, stirring constantly until mixture becomes one mass and lifts easily from bottom of pot. Remove from flame and cool. Form into little meat balls and dip in grated cheese or ground Brazilian nuts, walnuts or peanuts. Serve in paper patty shells.

LIVER PATÉ

⅔ *pound liver*
¼ *pound butter*
3 *whole eggs*
  salt and black pepper to taste
  ground nutmeg
  parsley and onion, chopped
1 *tablespoon mustard*
1 *cup milk*
1 *tablespoon flour*

PUT the liver through a meat grinder. Then combine with the butter and salt to taste. Place the milk, eggs, flour, nutmeg and black pepper in blender and mix well. Add the mixture to the liver and mix well. Place in greased dish and cook in double boiler.

LIVER PATÉ PATTIES

> *1 can liver paté*
> *1 egg*
> *½ cup flour*
> *1 teaspoon powder*
> *½ cup milk*
> *2 tablespoons grated Parmesan cheese*
> *bread crumbs*
> *salt to taste*

BEAT the egg and add the flour, cheese, milk, salt and baking powder. Mix well and then add the paté. Blend well and form into little balls. Roll the balls in the bread crumbs and fry.

"CUSCUZINHOS" IN A POT
(Shrimp Corn Muffins)

1 pound yellow corn flour
¼ pound manioc flour*
1 can hearts of palm*
2 pounds fresh shrimp
garlic pressed in salt
1 can sardines
3 hardboiled eggs, sliced
½ pound green olives, pitted
½ pound lard
1 pound tomatoes, chopped
1 large onion
parsley chopped fine
hot peppers

PLACE in a blender the tomatoes, the onion, hot peppers, parsley, garlic pressed in salt and 2 cups of water. Blend and then strain. Heat the lard, and when very hot, sauté the shrimp, chopped in small pieces. (Leave some of the shrimp aside for garnishing later.) Brown, then add in the blended mixture and simmer a while. Next add in the hearts of palm, cut in small pieces, together with the olives. When all ingredients are well cooked and the mixture has thickened, add the corn flour and manioc flour, stirring rapidly so that the mixture blends evenly. Continue stirring until the "cuscuz"* has enough consistency to lift easily from the bottom of the pot. Remove from heat. Grease a muffin tin or other desired

---

* See "Glossary for Cooks" on page 247.

baking form. At the bottom of each form, place minced pieces of egg, sardine, olive and shrimp. Pour in the "cuscuz" while still warm, fill to the top and press down to give it shape. When cool, turn out the "cuscuzinhos" with the aid of a knife and place each in a fancy paper pastry shell. These "cuscuzinhos" are excellent for a special festive table.

SHRIMP TIDBITS

6 cups milk
½ pound grated Parmesan cheesee
1 pound dried, ground shrimp
6 eggs
½ pound flour
   lemon juice drops, to taste
2 heaping tablespoons butter
1 cup coconut milk
   hot peppers, salt and black pepper, to taste
1 grated onion
2 peeled tomatoes without seeds
   pressed garlic clove

HEAT one half the butter and sauté the onion, garlic, peppers, all finely chopped. Add the ground shrimp and simmer, adding a little water to cook the shrimp. When cooked, remove from flame and cool a little, adding the milk, coconut milk, cheese, flour, 1 tablespoon butter and, lastly, the eggs which have been beaten and strained. Mix very well and pour into a buttered muffin pan. Place and olive in the middle of each small form and bake in a hot oven. (Dough should not be too hard; if it is, add more milk.)

SHRIMP-FILLED MILK PASTRY TURNOVERS

2 cups milk
1 tablespoon butter
2 cups flour
  salt to taste
1 pound shrimp
5 eggs
1 onion
3 tomatoes
1 pound bread crumbs
  hot peppers
  oil or lard to fry the turnovers

COMBINE the milk, butter and salt and bring to a boil. While the milk is boiling, add all of the flour immediately and stir rapidly to prevent lumping. Continue stirring until the mixture lifts easily from the bottom of the pan. Knead well and let stand for 20 minutes. In the meantime, sauté the onion, tomatoes and hot peppers, chopped fine and whatever other condiments desired. Next, add the shrimp and let sauté until tender. When the shrimp is ready, mash thoroughly with a fork or put through a blender. Add 2 egg yolks and 1 level tablespoon flour, mix well and heat until the mixture thickens.

Roll out the pastry dough and cut out in circles using a wide-mouthed cup. Place a heaping tablespoon of the shrimp filling in each pastry circle. Fold over each circle in half so that the edges meet and then flute the edges. Dip these turnovers in bread crumbs, then in the remaining eggs (lightly beaten) and then again in bread crumbs. Fry in lard or oil and serve while still warm.

PEPPER PATÉ

6 *red peppers*
6 *green peppers*
½ *pound grated Parmesan cheese*
2 *tablespoons butter*
1 *tablespoon mustard*
2 *eggs yolks*

BOIL the peppers in salted water. Drain off and mash through a fine strainer and cool. Add in the egg yolks and heat again, stirring continuously until mixture thickens and eggs are cooked. Remove from heat and cool. Add in the cheese, butter and mustard. Beat until mixture forms creamy paste. Hot peppers and black pepper may be added to taste.

RAISIN AND WALNUT SANDWICHES

1 *pound flour*
3 *yeast cakes*
1 *cup warm milk*
½ *pound butter*
4 *eggs, separated and beaten*
4 *medium size potatoes, cooked and puréed*
1 *tablespoon sugar*
1 *teaspoon salt*
½ *pound ham, ground and in strips*
⅔ *pound cheese, cut in fine strips*
¾ *pound seedless raisins*
½ *pound finely chopped walnuts*
⅓ *pound butter to brush on dough*

29

DISSOLVE the yeast in the warm milk and add the sugar, salt, beaten eggs, puréed potatoes, butter and, lastly, the sifted flour. Mix well. If mixture is too soft add a little more flour. After kneading the mixture, dab a little butter in openings within, fold over into 4 parts, and let stand for 15 minutes. Repeat this 3 times. Then divide the mixture in half and place one part in a greased baking dish. On top of this portion place the cheese strips, the strips of ham, and top with the raisins and nuts. Place the other portion over the first and cover with egg yolks combined with butter. Bake in a hot oven. Cool and cut into squares.

SOUPS

Ah, soup; beautiful soup!

When it comes time to settle down to the delightful business of dining, Brazilians invariably start their principal meal with a mouth-watering dish of soup. Some soups, in truth, are so rich —as you will find when, for example, you try the recipe for the vegetable soup— that they are almost a meal in themselves. The ones that follow are basic Brazilian recipes around which have been (and can be) built a thousand and one variations. But, first, try the original "themes" —they're too good to pass up.

....SOUPS..

BEEF BROTH STOCK

2 pounds stew beef
1 pound short ribs
1 pound meat bones
6 quarts water
2 tablespoons salt
4 onions
4 cloves garlic
1 large green pepper
1 bunch parsley
1 bay leaf
4 scallions

P LACE the meat and bones in a large pot with the water and put to boil. When the water begins to boil, remove the oily film that has formed on the top, add the 2 tablespoons salt and all the remaining ingredients, cut in medium size pieces. Cover and simmer over a very low flame for about 3 or 4 hours or until the meat has fallen off the short rib bones and can be cut with a spoon or fork. Strain the liquid. This broth is delicious by itself or can be used as the stock for many other soups and dishes requiring liquid.

BLACK BEAN SOUP

1 cup black beans
4 cups beef broth stock
  ham bone (optional)
1 onion
2 tablespoons olive oil
½ hot sausage
  bay leaf
  salt to taste

SOAK beans overnight. On the following day, drain the beans and put in a pot to cook with the beef broth stock and ham bone. Separately, sauté the onion and sausage, both chopped fine, in the olive oil. When brown, add to the beans and beef broth. Cover and let simmer over a low flame for about 45 minutes stirring occasionally so that the beans do not stick to the bottom of the pot. Test for seasoning and to see if beans are tender. If necessary, add salt to taste and cook the beans a while longer (adding more hot broth if needed) until they are completely soft. Remove the ham bone and put the soup through a blender so that it is of a creamy consistency. Heat again and serve immediately. If desired, serve with crotons fried in butter.

Note: This soup may also be made with cooked or leftover beans. In that case, for every cup of beans, add 1½ cups broth and heat. Sauté the onion and sausage as before and add to the soup. Test for seasoning and add salt if needed. Let simmer another 20 minutes before putting through the blender. Serve as above.

CHICKEN SOUP BRAZILIAN STYLE

1 *medium size stewing chicken*
2 *quarts water*
½ *cup rice*
½ *small onion, chopped*
1 *clove garlic, minced*
1 *tomato, peeled and seedless, chopped*
  scallion and parsley sprig, chopped fine
1 *large carrot, diced*
  salt and black pepper to taste

Cut the chicken in parts and cook in salted water until the chicken is tender. Add all the remaining ingredients, cover and let simmer over a low flame for another 20 minutes or so, until the rice and carrots are cooked. Taste and add salt and pepper if needed. Serve the chicken separately.

CORN SOUP

1 *dozen ears corn*
2 *tablespoons butter*
2 *eggs yolks*
1 *cup milk*
½ *pound beef stock for soup*
¼ *pound lard*
1 *onion*
3 *tomatoes*
  salt and garlic to taste

35

HEAT the lard and sauté the tomatoes, onion and the garlic pressed with salt. Add in the meat and simmer. Add in 3 quarts water and continue cooking until about half the water evaporates and a desirable broth is formed. Meanwhile, grate the corn and mash through a strainer. Remove the beef broth from the heat when done and strain. Add the juice of the corn to the broth, together with butter and the egg yolks mixed in a little milk. Return to the heat and stir constantly until mixture thickens. Cook about ½ hour longer so that the corn is well cooked.

VEGETABLE SOUP

1 pound stew beef
2 potatoes, peeled and quartered
3 carrots, peeled and quartered
1 sweet potato, peeled and quartered
1 turnip, peeled and quartered
1 large onion, chopped
2 large celery stalks, diced
1 tablespoon salt
  black pepper to taste
1 tablespoon butter or olive oil

PLACE stew beef in a pot, add twice its volume in water and bring to a boil. When water is boiling, add the remaining ingredients. If there is not enough water to cover, add more boiling water. Cover and let simmer over a low flame until the meat and vegetables are completely cooked. Remove the meat when tender and put the vegetables through a sieve or in a blender. Return to the pot with the liquid and heat again, mixing well. When ready to serve, add the butter or olive oil. Serve the meat in the soup or separately as desired.

Note: Beef broth stock (see recipe on page 33) may be substituted for all or part of the water. In this case, do not add the salt and pepper until after you have tested for seasoning.

FISH DISHES

Brazil has exactly 4,889 miles of Atlantic coastline and 27,318 miles of navigable water ways of which, 1,700 miles belong to the awesome Amazon River. This means that Brazil also has a whale of a lot —and a varied lot, at that— of fish. And to match, the Brazilians have almost as many recipes starring fish and sea food —especially shrimp for which they have an inordinate fondness. The recipes in this and the following section on shrimp dishes are their most traditional, most delicious —most successful. You will find here many of the Afro-Indian dishes which have made Brazilian cooking internationally known.

Section Three

··FISH DISHES··

CODFISH "DONA IZAURA"

potatoes
carrots
turnips
cauliflower
green peppers
asparagus
(quantity of vegetables will depend upon number of
persons to be served)
6 eggs
1 pound codfish cooked
8 tomatoes
¼ pound olives
2 cups milk
scallion and parsley sprig
2 large onions, sliced
flour, sufficient for the amount of sauce
olive oil
1 tablespoon butter
salt, garlic, black pepper and hot peppers to taste

Cook the vegetables separately in salted water. Boil 4 eggs and set aside. Heat the oil in saucepan and sauté the onions, tomatoes, chopped, 1 bay leaf, hot peppers and rest of seasonings. Make a thick gravy, enough to fill the bottom of a pyrex baking dish. Then arrange 1 layer of the vegetables, the cooked codfish cut in fillets and the hardboiled eggs, sliced. Then arrange another layer of gravy, vegetables, codfish and eggs. On top add some olives.

To the water in which the fish was cooked, add the 2 cups of milk, 2 eggs yolks, 1 tablespoon butter and flour enough to make a thin white sauce. Heat and stir until cooked. Add in salt and pepper to taste. Cover entrée with this sauce and garnish dish with eggs, tomatoes and olives. Then sprinkle a little oil on top and bake in low oven for ½ hour. Serve hot.

GRANDMA'S CREAMED FISH

1 pound fish
tomatoes
onion
5 tablespoons flour
1½ cups milk
2 tablespoons butter
10 tablespoons grated Parmesan cheese
3 eggs
liquid in which fish cooked
garlic, salt and hot peppers to taste

SEASON the fish to taste and sauté well with whatever condiments desired. Strain the liquid and separate the fish so as to remove the bones. Dissolve 5 tablespoons flour in ½ cup of milk. Stir in 3 egg yolks. Then add this mixture to the cooked and strained liquid and return to heat in order to thicken. Stir in 2 tablespoons butter, 10 tablespoons grated cheese, and black pepper to taste. When the sauce is cooked, add in the pieces of fish and mix lightly so that the fish is evenly distributed in the mixture. Remove from heat and turn in the beaten egg whites. Beat lightly, arrange in a pyrex baking dish and garnish with tomato slices, a sprinkling of grated cheese and butter chips. Bake about 20 minutes and serve while very hot.

FISH FILLETS "PARAÍBA" STYLE

> 6½ pounds fish fillets
> 6 eggs, beaten until stiff
> flour
> oil
> lemon juice
> garlic, salt and black pepper to taste

SEASON the fish with salt, garlic pressed in salt and lemon juice, and marinate in this sauce for 2 hours. Then, remove the fish, dry thoroughly using a cloth napkin and dip each fillet in flour and then in beaten eggs. Fry a few fillets at a time in a little oil until done golden brown on both sides.

Note: For festive occasions, cut the fillets in small pieces so that they may be served as tidbits or hors d'oeuvres.

MARINATED FISH

1 fish, sliced
garlic pressed in salt, black pepper
and hot pepper to taste
juice of 1 lemon
½ cup vinegar
1 cup dendê oil or olive oil
3 onions, sliced
1 clove garlic, minced
4 tomatoes, peeled and finely chopped

SEASON the sliced fish with the lemon juice, salt, garlic, black pepper and hot peppers, finely chopped and let marinate in this sauce for 2 hours. Then, drain and fry in the oil, saving 4 tablespoons for later. Separately, sauté the onions, tomatoes and a minced clove of garlic in the 4 tablespoons of oil. Add the vinegar and the sauce in which the fish was seasoned and let simmer for another 5 minutes or so, taking care not to let the onion and garlic get too brown. Remove the sauté from the heat. Next, spread out the slices of fish in a pan and cover with the sauce. Put in the refrigerator until the next day. Then, garnish a deep platter with lettuce, arrange the fish slices on it, cover with the marinating sauce and serve cold.

FISH "MUQUECA"*

2 pounds fish
1 large onion
4 lemons, juiced
  coriander seeds, salt and hot peppers to taste
2 tablespoons dendê oil (or olive oil)
  milk of 1 coconut

GRATE the coconut and press the meat to squeeze out all the coconut milk. Strain and put this liquid aside. Add a little water to the pressed coconut meat and press out the milk again. The second liquid will be thinner than the first. Put this liquid aside, apart from the first. Next, make a sauce with the onion pressed with the salt and hot peppers, the tomatoes cut in slices, the coriander seeds and the juice of two lemons. After cleaning the fish and cutting it into slices, dip it in the remaining lemon juice and place it in the sauce. Fifteen minutes before serving, add the thinner coconut milk to fish in the sauce, heat and let boil. When almost ready, add the dendê (or olive) oil. When the fish is done, cover with the thicker coconut milk and serve.

---

* *Muqueca* is a typical dish from Northeastern Brazil with fish and oil as the principal ingredients. The fish is generally stewed or simmered with the condiments (or other ingredients desired) and the oil is added at the end for taste.

FISH "MUQUECA"* FROM BAHIA

4 pounds fish cut in fillets of medium thickness
1 pound onions
    plenty of coriander seeds and parsley
1 pound tomatoes
½ cup lemon juice
    salt, black pepper and hot peppers to taste
½ cup water
1 cup oil
½ cup dendê oil or olive oil

BLEND all condiments (onions, coriander seeds, parsley, tomatoes, lemon juice, peppers, salt and black pepper) in a blender and place in a bowl. Add the fish fillets and let stand for 2 hours. Just before serving, place all ingredients in a pan and heat over a high flame adding the cup of oil slowly and letting the mixture boil. When fish is almost cooked and the sauce a little evaporated, add the dendê oil or olive oil and continue boiling a little. Care should be taken to see that the fish does not overcook. Serve hot.

---

* See "Glossary for Cooks" on page 247.

FISH "MUQUECA"* WITH MANIOC FLOUR*

1 pound fish
2 tablespoons oil
1 onion
2 peeled tomatoes without seeds
  salt, garlic and hot peppers to taste
  coriander seeds
  parsley sprig
3 eggs
  manioc flour
  banana or kale leaves

COVER the fish with the oil and condiments and heat. When the fish is cooked, remove skin and bones, strain the liquid and combine the fish with 3 lightly beaten eggs. Then heat, stirring constantly so that the eggs do not lump. When the eggs are cooked, thicken the mixture with manioc flour until it reaches a consistency firm enough for stuffing the leaves. When the mixture is sufficiently thick, wrap in the banana or kale leaves and place in a hot oven to bake. When the leaves are dried and yellow, the "muqueca" is done.

---

* See "Glossary for Cooks" on page 247.

FISH IN WHITE SAUCE

2 *pounds halibut (or any other fish desired)*
1 *tablespoon butter*
lemon juice
garlic, salt and black pepper to taste
coriander seeds and bay leaf

CUT THE fish into fillets, bone and season with plenty of lemon juice, salt and pepper. Heat the butter and add the garlic, salt, peppers, bay leaf and coriander seeds. Then add the fish fillets and keep adding water a little at a time and turning the fish constantly so that it browns evenly and cooks. Remove from heat before the fish is completely cooked because it will finish cooking in the oven. Separately, make the white sauce recipe given below. When the sauce is ready, pour a little of it into a greased baking dish. Then arrange a layer of fish fillets on top, cover with a layer of sauce, then fish and so on, ending with a top layer of sauce. Bake for about 20 minutes in a moderate oven.

White Sauce

4 *tablespoons cornstarch or flour*
4 *cups milk*
4 *egg yolks*
2 *tablespoons butter*
salt and black pepper to taste

COMBINE the milk, flour and the egg yolks and pass through a fine strainer. Season with salt, black pepper and butter. Heat over a low flame, stirring constantly to avoid lumping, until the mixture cooks and forms a creamy sauce. When ready, remove from heat and use immediately. You may add some grated cheese or the milk from 1 coconut (see recipe on page 173) or both, if desired.

SALMON OR SARDINE PUDDING

½ pound bread or small loaf of French bread
1 cup milk
3 tablespoons grated cheese
1 sprig parsley, finely chopped
1 finely chopped onion
1 tablespoon tomato paste
3 eggs
* hot peppers, to taste*
1 can salmon or 2 cans sardines, without bones
1 cup peas, cooked or canned
1 level tablespoon baking powder
2 tablespoons bread crumbs

BRING milk to a boil and pour over the bread. Mix in blender together with the tomato paste. Remove and add the grated onion, parsley, the egg whites beaten lightly, the salmon or sardines and the peas. Butter a pyrex baking dish and sprinkle with bread crumbs. Pour in mixture and bake in moderate oven for about 30 minutes or until golden brown. Serve hot.

"SARAPATEL"* OF TURTLE FROM AMAZONAS

tripe, giblets and blood of turtle
bay leaf
lemon juice
tomatoes, peeled and seedless
onion
green pepper
garlic, salt, black pepper and hot chili pepper to taste
coriander seeds
lard

WASH the turtle giblets thoroughly in boiling water and lemon juice so that the skin may be more easily removed. After skin is removed, wash again in fresh water and more lemon juice. Cut into small pieces also adding in chopped pieces of the meat and some fat of the turtle. Season with salt and pressed garlic, black pepper, hot chili pepper, onion, tomatoes peeled and without seeds, green pepper, coriander seeds and bay leaf. Place all ingredients in a large pot, cover with water and cook until done, then add in the blood. Let boil a little longer so that it becomes consistent and serve hot over rice (see recipe on page 137).

---

* *Sarapatel* is a type of thick sauce or stew made with the coagulated blood, organs and meat of an animal such as the turtle, duck or pig, etc. It is invariably served with rice.

SHRIMP DISHES

························SHRIMP DISHES ························

SHRIMP ALAGOAS STYLE

2 *pounds fresh, large shrimp*
1 *pound fresh small shrimp*
1 *pint water*
5 *eggs*
  onion
  tomatoes
  garlic, salt and hot peppers to taste
  cooking oil
4 *tablespoons flour*

Do NOT cut off heads or tails of the large shrimp but only peel and clean. Boil in salted water, placing a heavy cover on top of the pan. Heat the oil and sauté the onion, tomatoes and other condiments which have been finely chopped. When brown, add in the small shrimp and a little water. When cooked, put the mixture through blender then add 1 pint milk, 2 egg yolks and 4 tablespoons flour. Salt to taste, return to heat and cook until mixture thickens. Cool, then wrap around each of the large shrimp, leaving the head and tail uncovered. Dip in bread crumbs, then in lightly beaten eggs and again in the bread crumbs. Fry and serve hot.

SHRIMP OR CHICKEN WITH CREAM CHEESE

¼ pound butter
1 onion
3 tomatoes
garlic, hot peppers and salt to taste
parsley sprig
1 cream cheese packet
1¼ pounds fresh shrimp or
small frying chicken

HEAT the butter and sauté shrimp with the onion, tomatoes, garlic, hot peppers and parsley, all finely chopped. If using chicken, sauté in the same fashion and add water, a little at a time, in order to cook the chicken and leave some broth. Cool and shred the chicken, removing the bones.

Line the bottom of a pyrex baking dish with the cream cheese. Add the sautéed shrimp or the chicken on top of the layer of cream cheese and bake enough to melt the cheese and make a sauce. Serve hot.

SHRIMP CROQUETTES

1 *pound shrimp*
2 *tomatoes*
1 *onion*
  garlic, salt and hot peppers to taste
¼ *pound butter*
  lard or oil for frying
  scallion and parsley sprig
  milk
  green peppers
2 *egg yolks*
3 *whole eggs*
  flour
  bread crumbs

HEAT the butter and sauté the shrimp with the tomatoes, onion and condiments, all chopped fine. When brown, add a little milk in which 2 egg yolks have been mixed lightly, and enough flour to thicken the mixture and give it sufficient consistency to form croquettes. While cooking, stir constantly to avoid lumps. When mixture thickens enough to lift easily from bottom of pot, remove from heat and cool. Then form into croquettes and dip in beaten eggs, then bread crumbs and fry in lard or oil.

"CUSCUZ"* WITH SHRIMP SÃO PAULO STYLE

> 2 *pounds fresh shrimp*
> 1 *pound yellow corn flour*
> 1 *onion*
> *salt and black pepper to taste*
> 4 *cloves garlic*
> *scallion and parsley sprig*
> ⅔ *pound lard (or other shortening)*
> 1 *pound tomatoes*
> 1 *sweet green pepper*
> 1 *can hearts of palm***
> 1 *can small peas*
> ¼ *pound manioc flour***
> ½ *pound olives, chopped*
> 3 *hardboiled eggs*

HEAT one half of the lard or oil and sauté the onion chopped fine, with the salt, garlic, black pepper and hot peppers. Add in the tomatoes and the green pepper which have been liquefied in a blender together with a little water. Bring the sautéed mixture to a boil and when boiling, add in the shrimp which have been cleaned and halved, but leave out a few shrimp to use as garnish later. Cut the hearts of palm into medium size pieces and add to the shrimp mixture together with 1¼ cups of water. When the mixture boils and the liquid has thickened, add in the peas and chopped olives.

---

* *Cuscuz* is a type of pudding made with corn flour, rice flour, manioc flour or tapioca, often combined with many different ingredients.
**See "Glossary for Cooks" on page 247.

56

This shrimp mixture should have plenty of liquid remaining so that the "cuscuz" does not become too dry.

Separately, combine 1 pound yellow corn flour, manioc flour and a little salt and mix well. Add the parsley and scallion chopped fine. Heat the remaining lard until it melts and is so hot that it bubbles and then pour over the flour mixture. Mix well with a wooden spoon so that the lard is completely dispersed throughout the flour mixture and the flour is "scalded." To this scalded flour, add the shrimp mixture which, at this point, should be ready, and two of the hardboiled eggs, chopped fine. (Save an egg for garnishing later.) If the mixture is too soft, add a little more corn flour. (To tell if the "cuscuz" mixture is of the right consistency, put a little of it in the palm of your hand and press the point of a knife into it, clenching your fist. If on withdrawing the knife, it comes out clean, the mixture is ready.)

Garnish the bottom and sides of a deep pan or pudding form with hearts of palm and shrimp and slices of hardboiled egg, olives and tomatoes. (This pan must be able to fit into the top part of the "cuscuzeiro"*.) Boil water in the lower part of the "cuscuzeiro" and place the pan with the "cuscuz" (which has been covered with a moistened cloth napkin) on top of the "cuscuzeiro" tray. Cover the "cuscuzeiro" and place over a low flame to simmer. In about

---

* A "cuscuzeiro" is a type of pot, similar to a "Dutch oven," which the Brazilian housewife uses to cook her "cuscuz" dishes. The "cuscuzeiro" consists of a lower part in which water is boiled. This lower part is separated from the upper part by a tray having many small holes which permit the steam created by the boiling water to pass through to the upper portion of the "cuscuzeiro." The upper portion, in turn, fits snugly in to the tray and has its own tight-fitting cover.

two hours, when the steam has penetrated the "cuscuz," cooking the corn flour batter, and the cloth napkin is more or less dry, the "cuscuz" will be ready. At this point, remove from the heat and let cool slightly before turning on a platter which has been garnished with lettuce, hardboiled eggs and olives. When the "cuscuz" is turned, the hearts of palm, shrimp, sliced eggs, tomatoes and olives will now appear as a decorative topping.

SHRIMP "FRITADA"* FROM BAHIA

1 pound shrimp
1 can peas
5 eggs
   milk of 1 coconut
   hot peppers
   oil
   onion
   tomatoes
   parsley
   coriander seeds
   garlic pressed in salt

PEEL and wash the shrimp thoroughly. In the oil, sauté the onion, tomatoes, parsley and coriander seeds, all chopped fine, the garlic

---

* *Fritada* is a typically Brazilian dish in which the principal ingredients have been chopped or minced, mixed with beaten eggs and then baked in the oven until golden brown. The ingredients can include such things as pieces of fish, shrimp, potatoes, vegetables, etc., which have been seasoned as desired. *Fritada,* in short is a glorified, but delicious deep-dish omelet.

pressed with salt and the hot peppers. Then add in the shrimp, simmering for a few minutes. Remove pan from heat and add in the milk from 1 coconut† together with 2 tablespoons of oil and 1 can of peas. Return pan to heat and stir constantly. Pour 5 beaten eggs over the top and when the eggs are cooked, place the "fritada" in the oven until lightly browned. After the eggs have been poured on top, do not mix but shake the pan slightly, spreading the eggs evenly over the top, so that the "fritada" browns evenly.

SHRIMP AND CORN "FRITADA"*

5 ears corn or 1 can corn
5 eggs
scallion and paraley sprig
grated onion
salt and pepper to taste
½ pound large, fresh shrimp
3 tablespoons butter

CUT OFF the kernels from the ears of corn and wash thoroughly. If using canned corn, drain of liquid and rinse in hot water. Cook the corn kernels in boiling, salted water and when done, drain. Heat butter in a frying pan and when golden brown in color, add the shrimp, which have been thoroughly washed and seasoned in lemon juice, salt and black pepper. Keep turning so that the shrimp brown evenly. When they begin to turn golden brown, add the corn kernels and the grated onion. A little of the water in

---

† See recipe on page 173.
* See "Glossary for Cooks" on page 247.

which the corn was cooked may be added to make the shrimp more tender, if desired.

Grease a deep baking dish and pour in the shrimp and corn mixture. Beat the egg whites until stiff and then fold in the yolks, the parsley and scallion chopped fine, and a pinch of salt and pepper. Spread over the shrimp and corn mixture in the baking dish, mix lightly with a fork and bake. When it is browned and of firm consistency, the "fritadas" is ready to serve.

CREAMED SHRIMP WITH HEARTS OF PALM*

1 can hearts of palm
2 pounds fresh shrimp
1 onion
1 tomato
3 tablespoons tomato sauce
1 cup of cornstarch
green pepper
parsley and bay leaf
stuffed olives
salt, black pepper and hot peppers to taste
olive oil

SAUTÉ the onion, tomato, hot and green peppers and parsley, all chopped fine, and the shrimp in olive oil. Add salt and pepper and the tomato sauce mixed in a cup of water. When these ingredients

---

* See "Glossary for Cooks" on page 247.

are cooked and a broth formed, strain the mixture and set the liquid aside to cool. Add to it a cup of cornstarch mixing constantly so it will blend evenly. Combine the cornstarch mixture with the shrimp mixture and let cook over a low flame, stirring constantly, until mixture thickens and forms a cream. Add to this cream the hearts of palm, which, when taken from the can, should immediately be dipped in lemon juice so they do not become dark. Olives, preferably stuffed, may be added.

Note: Do not cook this mixture more than five minutes. This recipe may also be used as a filler for pies or the creamed shrimp may be served with rice (see recipe on page 137) or over toast.

SHRIMP WITH HEARTS OF PALM*

2 pounds fresh shrimp
1 can hearts of palm
1 onion
4 tablespoons olive oil
1 tomato
2 tablespoons lemon juice
1 small green pepper, sliced
*   parsley sprig and bay leaf*
*   salt and pepper to taste*

Sauté the onion, tomato, green pepper and parsley, all chopped fine in the 4 tablespoons of olive oil. When the sauté is ready, add

---

* See "Glossary for Cooks" on page 247.

the shrimp, which should be cleaned beforehand in water and lemon juice, and let simmer until tender. When the shrimp is cooked, add the hearts of palm, cut in medium size pieces, and cook 2 or 3 minutes longer—just enough to heat the hearts of palm. Serve immediately with rice (see recipe on page 137).

SHRIMP LASAGNA BRAZILIAN STYLE

>*4 cups flour*
>*4 eggs*
>*4 tablespoons spinach juice*
>*1 teaspoon salt dissolved in juice*
>*⅔ pound butter*
>*3 cups milk*
>*⅓ pound tomatoes*
>*2 pounds fresh shrimp*
>*3 egg yolks*
>*"ricotta" or pot cheese*
>*2 tablespoons flour*
>*onion*
>*garlic, salt, hot peppers, to taste*
>*1 scallion and a sprig of parsley,*
>*minced and mashed together*

Cook some leaves of spinach in a little water. When cooked, blend in liquefier with salt, strain, measure out 4 tablespoons and combine with flour which has been sifted into a bowl. Add the eggs and 1 teaspoon of butter. Knead well. If the dough sticks to the hands, pat on a little more flour. Knead again and roll out into a slightly

62

thinner than regular thickness. Let dry a little and cut into wide strips about 4″ long by 2″ wide. Put on a pot of water to boil with a little salt. When the water is boiling vigorously, put in the noodle strips to cook. Boil as desired: either al dente or until the dough is soft. When ready, use a straining spoon to dip out the noodles a few at a time. Place on a cloth napkin separately so they do not stick together. Do this rapidly while they are still hot. The shrimp sauce and cheese sauce (see below) should be readied beforehand so that the dish can be prepared while the noodles are still hot and easy to work with.

Shrimp Sauce

Heat half of the butter and when brown, add the shrimp cut into small pieces. (The shrimp should be left marinating in lemon juice and salt for some time before use.) Brown the shrimp a little then add hot peppers, garlic, onion and tomatoes which have been mixed in the blender. Add salt to taste and simmer. 1 bay leaf may also be added.

Cheese Sauce

Combine the milk, 2 tablespoons flour, the cheese and egg yolks in a bowl. Mix well and strain. Place mixture in pot and heat, adding butter and a little black pepper. Mix constantly to avoid sticking and cook well. When it is cooked and thickened, remove from heat.

Select a large, deep pyrex baking dish and arrange in layers starting with the cheese sauce, then strips of dough in criss-cross fashion so that it will be easier to cut. Follow with the shrimp sauce, then another layer of dough, then cheese sauce and continue like this until finished. The top layer should be cheese sauce and shrimp sauce mixed lightly with a fork. Sprinkle with grated cheese and bake in a hot oven about 30 minutes.

SHRIMP MOUSSE

1 quart milk
1 small jar pickles
1 pound fresh shrimp
1 pound peeled tomatoes without seeds
4 tablespoons cornstarch
1 onion, grated
nutmeg
1 bay leaf
salt and garlic to taste
parsley sprig
2 lemons, juiced
2 tablespoons vinegar
2 tablespoons olive oil
2 packages of unflavored gelatin

HEAT the oil and sauté grated onion, salt, pressed garlic, bay leaf, a little nutmeg and the tomatoes, chopped. Add in the shrimp, cleaned and cut into small pieces. Add a little water and simmer until the shrimp is cooked. When this sauté is ready, remove the bay leaf.

Using another pan, boil the heads of the shrimp in a little water. When done, strain and press in order to obtain a maximum amount of liquid. Add this liquid to the shrimp mixture and cook until some liquid has evaporated. Then slowly add in the milk into which the cornstarch has been dissolved. Continue adding in the milk and cornstarch until a thick cream has formed. Then add in the lemon juice, vinegar, pickles, chopped fine and, lastly, the gelatin dissolved in a little boiling water. Mix well and then remove from heat. (The consistency of the cream may be tested by putting a little of it into cold water. If it hardens immediately it is done. If not, return to heat and add a little more milk and cornstarch. The exact amount of milk and cornstarch needed depends upon the amount of sauce resulting from the sautéed shrimp, lemon juice, vinegar and gelatin. Therefore, it is important to test the consistency of the cream or "mousse.") Using oil, grease a large baking pan and pour in the "mousse." Chill and turn out when ready to serve.

THE "MUQUECA"* I LIKE

1 pound chicken giblets
1 pound fresh shrimp
1 cup olive oil
2 cups yellow corn flour or manioc flour
   hot peppers
1 pound tomatoes
2 onions
   salt and garlic to taste
   scallion and parsley sprig
   coriander seeds

---

* See "Glossary for Cooks" on page 247.

SAUTÉ the chicken giblets with the condiments and the oil. Then add enough water to cook. Simmer, remove from heat and strain. Chop the giblets in small pieces and add the shrimp. Combine with the strained gravy and heat. When the shrimp is cooked, thicken the mixture slowly with the yellow corn flour or manioc flour,** stirring constantly to avoid lumping. When the mixture has enough consistency to lift easily from the bottom of the pot, remove from heat and serve immediately. This "muqueca" should not be too thick. Serve with rice (see recipe on page 137).

"CARURÚ"* FROM BAHIA
(Shrimp and Okra Dish)

    2 pounds shrimp
    1 pound okra, fresh or frozen
      black pepper and hot peppers to taste
      manioc flour
    4 tablespoons dendê oil or olive oil

COOK the 1 pound of okra, sliced, in boiling, salted water. When cooked, drain in order to remove some of the gummy residue. Sauté the shrimp with plenty of hot peppers and with all the condiments desired. Then add in the okra. Simmer a little, slowly adding enough manioc flour** to thicken the mixture. When ready

---

* *Carurú* is a dish which came to Brazil by way of Sudan in Africa. The principal ingredients are shrimp, okra and dendê oil, with many variations built around this theme.

** See "Glossary for Cooks" on page 247.

to serve, add in the dendê or olive oil and do not let boil. Serve with "angú" made with rice flour rather than corn flour (see recipe on page 139).

"CARURÚ" FROM MURITIBA
(Shrimp and Okra Dish)

1 pound small tender okra
1 pound dried shrimp
1 onion, grated
  milk of 1 coconut
  dendê oil or olive oil
  salt, garlic, coriander seeds, and hot peppers to taste

CUT the okra into small pieces, rinse in water and lemon juice, drain and dry in order to remove the gummy substance. Combine with the shrimp, which have been soaked in water, drained, cleaned and ground. Add the grated onion, garlic pressed with salt, peppers and coriander seeds, chopped fine. Combine all ingredients (except the oil) in a pot, heat and add in the milk of 1 coconut† and a little water. Cook over a medium flame, stirring occasionally until the mixture lifts easily from the bottom of the pot. Add dendê or olive oil as desired and mix well. Serve hot and, in the tureen in which the "carurú"* is served, add a little dendê or olive oil when ready to serve.

---

* See "Glossary for Cooks" on page 247.
† See recipe on page 173.

67

ONIONS STUFFED WITH SHRIMP

6 *large Spanish onions*
1½ *cups fresh shrimp*
  olive oil
  garlic pressed in salt
  black pepper and hot peppers to taste
  scallion and parsley sprig, chopped fine
2 *tablespoons butter*
  manioc flour or flour
3 *tomatoes, chopped*
1 *tablespoon white wine*
½ *cup water*
  "farofa" or buttered bread crumbs
  grated Parmesan cheese

PEEL and boil the onions in salted water until tender. Meanwhile, sauté the shrimp in the olive oil along with the garlic, salt, tomatoes, scallion, parsley, black pepper and hot peppers, minced. When the shrimp is tender, remove from heat and mash and mix well or put through a blender. When the onions are ready remove the pulp from the center and stuff with the shrimp mixure. In a separate saucepan, melt the butter and sauté the onion pulp, slowly adding about 2 tablespoons manioc flour and salt to taste. Stir constantly so that it browns evenly and does not burn. Next add the wine and water, mixing well and letting simmer for about 5 minutes until the sauce thickens. Place onions in a baking dish and cover with the sauce. Top with "farofa" (see recipe on page 135) or buttered bread crumbs and the grated Parmesan cheese and bake in a moderate oven for about 10 minutes until golden.

SHRIMP PIE "BOSSANOVA"

1 loaf white bread, unsliced
1 pound shrimp
½ pound liver paste
½ pound walnuts, ground
½ pound ham, ground
1 tablespoon butter
mayonnaise
tomate paste*
parsley, chopped

TRIM the bread and slice lengthwise into 5 slices. Spread a little mayonnaise on each slice. On the first slice add ⅔ pound shrimp, sautéed and ground. Cover with the 2nd slice which has been covered with the liver paste mixed with finely chopped parsley. Cover with the 3rd slice which has been spread with a mixture of the ground ham, butter and ground walnuts. Spread the 4th slice with the tomato paste or any other desired filling and cover with the last slice. Cover entire loaf with mayonnaise and garnish as desired, using the remainder of the shrimp, whole. Chill and serve.

----

* See recipe on page 167.

SHRIMP PIE "LUIZ"

1 pound flour
½ teaspoon salt
1 whole egg and 1 egg yolk
1 tablespoon butter
1 cup milk
¼ pound grated cheese

To make dough sift 1 pound flour with ½ teaspoon salt. Add in 1 whole egg and 1 tablespoon butter and 1 cup milk. Knead and form into ball. Let stand 1 hour. Then, roll out ½ of the dough and line the bottom of a greased pie pan. Place the shrimp filling (see recipe below) on top and cover with the rest of the dough, fluting the edges with a fork. Brush with egg yolk mixed with butter and then sprinkle with grated cheese. Bake in medium oven.

Shrimp Filling

1 pound shrimp
3 tomatoes
1 onion
scallion and parsley sprig
1 egg yolk
1 can hearts of palm*
1 can peas
¼ pound flour
1 tablespoon butter

---

* See "Glossary for Cooks" on page 247.

Heat 1 tablespoon butter. Add the onion, condiments desired and tomatoes, all chopped fine, and sauté. Then add in the shrimp, hearts of palm, sliced, and 4 cups water. Simmer a while then add in the peas and the scallion and parsley, chopped fine. Boil and thicken with a little flour and 1 egg yolk. Stir until a cream sauce forms. Cool and use.

SHRIMP PIE "MOLITERNO"

1 pound flour
1 yeast cake
1 cup warm milk
1 level tablespoon salt
½ teaspoon sugar
5 eggs, beaten
2 tablespoons butter
1 tablespoon lard, melted
¾ pound bland cheese in strips
½ pound grated Parmesan cheese

Melt the yeast, sugar and 1½ cups flour in the warm milk. Let stand for 40 minutes. Then add the beaten eggs, the butter, lard and salt. Knead well until dough is smooth. Butter a baking dish. Divide the dough into two parts. Roll out one part with the rolling pin and line the baking dish. Pour in half of the shrimp sauce, made from recipe given on the following page.

When shrimp mixture has been poured into baking dish lined with dough, place on top of the mixture half of the cheese strips and sprinkle with grated cheese. Cover with the other half of dough and reverse the procedure—first place the cheese strips on the dough, then the rest of the shrimp mixture and sprinkle with grated cheese and place pieces of butter on top. Let stand another 20 minutes. Then place in hot oven to bake for 30 to 40 minutes.

Shrimp Sauce

1 pound tomatoes, peeled and seedless
2 pounds shrimp
1 onion
1 cup water
   garlic, hot peppers, salt to taste
   parsley sprig and scallion
   butter to fry the shrimp

CLEAN and wash shrimp in water and lemon juice. Place the onion, peppers, tomatoes, parsley sprig and scallion, and the cup water in blender. When thoroughly blended, add the shrimp. Turn the blender on and off 3 times in rapid succession so that the shrimp become more or less broken up. Heat a little butter and when brown, add the shrimp mixture with salt and pepper to taste. Simmer long enough to cook the shrimp and to let the mixture become thick. When ready, remove from heat, let cool and pour into pastry shell.

SHRIMP PUDDING FROM BAHIA

1 grated coconut
2 cups milk
1 loaf white bread (½ pound)
5 eggs
1 pound shrimp
¼ pound grated Parmesan cheese
¼ pound butter
salt, hot peppers and black pepper to taste
parsley sprig and scallion
coriander seeds

GRATE the coconut meat. Then bring milk to a boil and mix with the grated coconut. Strain this mixture through a moist linen napkin and squeeze thoroughly so that all the coconut milk is drained out. Trim the bread and soak in milk mixture for a few hours. Meanwhile, sauté the shrimp in the butter with all the condiments (to taste). When the bread has thoroughly soaked, put in blender with 5 egg yolks. Remove and then add the egg whites, beaten until fluffy, and the sautéed shrimp, the grated cheese and the hot peppers. Mix ingredients well and bake in greased pyrex baking dish in a hot oven. When done (to find out, test with a toothpick), turn out and garnish with lettuce leaves, sliced hard-boiled eggs, etc.

"EFÓ" FROM BAHIA
(Shrimp with Spinach)

1 pound dried shrimp, ground
1 pound fresh shrimp
1 pound spinach
1 cup dendê oil or olive oil
1 onion
3 tomatoes
2 green peppers
garlic, salt, black pepper and hot peppers to taste
coriander seeds to taste

HEAT the oil and sauté the onion, tomatoes, green peppers, garlic, salt and hot peppers. When done, strain. Return the strained liquid to the pot and heat, adding the dried shrimp, which have been soaked overnight in water in order to remove the salt, then washed well and put through a meat grinder. Also add the fresh shrimp and simmer, stirring occasionally in order not to burn. Cook the spinach in boiling salted water. Place the spinach in blender with a little of the juice in which it was cooked. When blended, add to the shrimp mixture and cook well adding a little dendê oil. Stir occasionally and let mixture thicken a little. (It should not be too thick. To thin add more oil.) After cooking there is always a little water on top of the "efó." Therefore add a little manioc flour* until the water disappears. Serve this typical dish from Bahia with coconut rice. (See recipe on page 138).

---

* See "Glossary for Cooks" on page 247.

OLD FASHIONED "VATAPÁ"*

*2 pounds dried shrimp
onion
salt, garlic and hot peppers to taste
dendê oil or olive oil
1 loaf white bread
½ pound peanuts, unsalted
milk of 1 coconut*

CLEAN the dried shrimp thoroughly. Then put through meat grinder together with the onion, salt, garlic and hot peppers. Sauté this mixture in a little dendê or olive oil and simmer. Then add the loaf of bread, trimmed, which has been soaked in water and blended with the milk of 1 coconut.† Bring the mixture to a boil, stirring constantly to avoid sticking. Then add in the roasted peanuts, shelled and ground, and then a little oil. Remove from heat and serve with creamed rice or rice flour "angú" (recipe on page 139). The "vatapá" is done when a crust has been formed or the mixture can be easily lifted from the bottom of the pot.

---

* Vatapá is another one of those delicious dishes which came to Brazil by way of Africa. Its main ingredients are shrimp or fish (or occasionally fowl), coconut milk, dendê oil and some kind of flour.
† See recipe on page 173.

"VATAPÁ"* OF FISH

1 *pound peeled, dried shrimp*
2 *pounds fish (as desired)*
2 *pounds fresh shrimp*
½ *pound roasted peanuts, shelled*
¾ *pound rice flour or white flour*
  milk of 1 coconut
1 *pound tomatoes*
1 *or 2 cups dendê oil or olive oil to taste*
onion
scallion and parsley sprig
hot peppers, black pepper, garlic and salt to taste

SAUTÉ the tomatoes, onion, scallion and parsley sprig, all chopped fine. Add the black pepper and garlic, minced and pressed in salt, to taste. Mix well and separate the sautéed mixture into two parts. In one part, sauté the fresh shrimp, first setting aside the heads and shell. In the second part, sauté the fish, cut in medium size pieces. Wash the dried shrimp thoroughly and sauté along with the fresh shrimp. Next, separate 15 shrimp heads and toast in the oven until lightly browned. (Don't allow the heads to brown too much.) Boil the remaining shrimp heads and shells. Grind the peanuts, toasted shrimp heads and hot peppers and add to the boiling shrimp heads and shells. Boil well, strain and add the sautéed shrimp and fish to the strained liquid. Thicken the mixture with the flour, mixing continuously so as not to lump. When ready to serve, add coconut milk (page 173) and dendê (or olive) oil.

---

* See "Glossary for Cooks" on page 247.

LITTLE JULIA'S "VATAPÁ"*

The following recipe is for 10 persons.

4¼ pounds fresh shrimp
4¼ pounds fish without bones
1 onion, chopped fine
2 cloves garlic
4¼ pounds tomatoes
1 pound manioc flour* or plain flour
milk of 2 coconuts
2 cups dendê oil (or olive oil)
hot peppers and black peppers to taste
1 cup olive oil

HEAT 1 cup olive oil and sauté the chopped onion and pressed garlic. When brown, add in the shrimp and fish. Brown a little then add in the tomatoes which have been blended with a little water. Let simmer until the shrimp and fish are cooked. Then, slowly sprinkle in the sifted manioc flour, or flour, until mixture thickens to desired consistency. Continue to cook a little longer, stirring constantly. Lastly, add in the coconut milk† and the dendê oil. Remove from flame and serve while very hot, with creamed rice.

NOTE: ground roasted peanuts and cashew nuts may be added also. It is best to grind the nuts in a nutmeg grinder or cheese grater.

---

* See "Glossary for Cooks" on page 247.
† See recipe on page 173.

77

"FRITADA"* OF CRABS FROM PARAÍBA

> 6 large crabs
> milk from 1 coconut
> 4 eggs, beaten until stiff
> 4 medium size potatoes
> coriander seeds
> 1 medium size onion
> 2 carrots
> 1 can peas
> ½ cup olive oil
> 2 peeled tomatoes without seeds
> 1 green pepper

WASH the crabs thoroughly and boil in salted water for ½ hour. Drain and remove the meat using a nutcracker and hammer to break the shell. Heat the oil and sauté the tomatoes, onion, coriander seeds and green pepper, all chopped fine. Add in the crab meat, potatoes and carrots, which have been cooked and chopped. Add the can of peas, and milk from 1 coconut.† Simmer until some of the liquid has evaporated. Remove from heat, place in a pyrex baking dish and cover with the beaten eggs which have been lightly salted. Bake in a hot oven about 15 minutes or until brown.

NOTE: This dish may also be used substituting shrimp, ground codfish fillets or any white fish.

---

* See "Glossary for Cooks" on page 247.
† See recipe on page 173.

SEA FOOD "FRITADA"* FROM ESPÍRITO SANTO

fresh shrimp
mussels and clams
fish
onions
tomatoes, peeled and seedless
coriander seeds
juice of 1 lemon
olive oil
whole eggs
salt and black pepper
garlic pressed in salt
hot peppers

This dish should be prepared in a clay pot. It is traditionally served during Holy Week. If a clay pot is not available it may also be prepared in an ordinary pot.

Thoroughly wash the mussels and clams in water, salt and lemon juice and clean well. Heat the oil and when very hot, sauté the shrimp, the mussels, the fish which have been cut in medium size pieces and boned. Leave on the flame until the ingredients begin to brown. Then add in the onion, chopped fine, some tomatoes, also chopped in small pieces, coriander seeds, lemon juice and the hot peppers. When mixture is brown and tender, place in a pyrex baking dish, cover with eggs beaten whole and bake until brown.

---

* See "Glossary for Cooks" on page 247.

MEAT DISHES

"God sends meat —and the Devil sends cooks," said John Taylor, an Englishman. But, then, the English cooks are notorious for their boiled beef and fried steaks. Who could blame Mr. Taylor? The pity is he never tried beef Brazilian style.

God did send the Brazilians meat: Brazil has among the world's largest herds of cattle and swine. Only India and the United States (in that order) have more head of cattle; only the U.S. and Russia have more swine.

The devil, however, doesn't come into the picture at all. The Brazilians are natural-born cooks. You will find no diabolical influences in the recipes that follow. As a matter of fact, you might say most of them are plainly heaven-sent, too.

83

·· MEAT DISHES ····································

"ANGÚ PAULISTA"
(São Paulo Corn Mush with Pork and Creamed Vegetables)

1 pound pork
1 pound tomatoes, peeled and seedless
½ quart milk
2 tablespoons butter
1 tablespoon lard
yellow corn meal (as needed)
½ pound bland cheese, cut in fine slices
¼ pound grated cheese
½ small cauliflower, cooked
1 can hearts of palm*
2 grated carrots
2 tablespoons cornstarch
1 onion
garlic pressed with salt

Boil 1 quart of salted water with just enough salt to taste. When boiling, add 1 tablespoon butter and then slowly keep adding the

---

* See "Glossary for Cooks" on page 247.

yellow corn meal until mixture thickens. Lower flame and continue cooking for ½ hour, stirring occasionally so that the corn mush does not stick and cooks thoroughly. It should be thick but not too firm. Put the pork through the meat grinder and sauté together with the onion, lard, the tomatoes, chopped fine, the salt, garlic and enough water so that there will be plenty of gravy. Let boil for a time until a thick sauce is formed. Remove from flame and put aside. Heat the milk with a little salt, 1 tablespoon butter and the grated cheese. Add the hearts of palm, chopped, the cauliflower, which should have been cooked and cut into small pieces, and the 2 grated carrots. Thicken this mixture with the white cornstarch which has been dissolved in a little milk. Mix well and stir continuously to avoid lumping. When thick and well cooked, remove from heat. Arrange ingredients in layers in a large pyrex dish starting with a layer of the corn mush, then the meat sauce, then strips of cheese and then cover with the creamed vegetables. Sprinkle some grated cheese on top and bake in a hot oven for a few minutes, just enough to brown.

DRIED BEEF BALLS FROM RIO GRANDE

1 pound dried beef
scallion and parsley sprig
hot peppers
tomatoes
2 eggs
flour
butter
oil for frying

PLACE the dried beef in hot water and soak overnight. The next day, drain off, wash the meat thoroughly and put through a meat grinder. Heat the butter and sauté the onion, scallion, tomatoes and a few hot peppers, all chopped fine. Then, add the dried beef and let fry a little. Remove from heat and add 1 egg yolk and 2 tablespoons flour. Return to heat and stir continuously until the mixture sticks together and lifts easily from the bottom of the pot. Remove and cool. Then form into little balls and fry in hot lard or oil. Make a gravy with tomatoes, onion, garlic, etc. and add the fried beef balls. Return again to the fire so that the sauce penetrates the meat. Serve very hot.

"PAÇOCA DO NORTE"
(Dried Beef with "Farofa")

>2 pounds of dried beef
>3 cups toasted manioc flour* or toasted corn flour
>½ pound lard
>2 onions
>salt and hot peppers to taste

SOAK the meat in water overnight to take out the salt and to make it more tender. Heat the lard and sauté the onions and the hot peppers, chopped fine. Fry a little. Add the meat, well washed and chopped in small pieces. Simmer for a little while until evenly browned, adding a little water to make the meat tender. When golden brown, remove from flame and put through a meat grinder

---

* See "Glossary for Cooks" on page 247

twice so that the meat is well shredded. While grinding, add the toasted flour little by little. After a while, the meat should be throughly mixed with the flour, forming a crumbly mixture. When ready, serve immediately.

MOCK BEEF PATTIES "CARIOCA" STYLE

1 pound meat, ground
2 eggs (1 whole and 1 yolk)
2 heaping tablespoons flour
1 grated onion
chopped parsley sprig
4 grated carrots
garlic pressed in salt
few drops lemon juice
hot peppers, minced

PUT MEAT through a meat grinder and then combine with the eggs, flour, onion, carrots, parsley, salt and hot peppers to taste. Mix thoroughly and add in a few drops lemon juice. Then form into a compact mixture. Flour a rolling board and knead the mixture. Flatten out to a thickness of about ⅜ inch, press together firmly and then, using a glass or cup, cut out the patties. Dip in sifted flour and fry in hot lard or oil. Serve with plenty of tomato sauce.

SÃO PAULO ROLLED BEEF WITH "FAROFA"

3½ pounds round steak, sliced thin
¼ pound olives, chopped fine
3 tablespoons butter
2 hardboiled eggs, chopped fine
¼ pound seedless raisins, chopped fine
    scallion and parsley sprig, chopped fine
    minced garlic, salt and black pepper to taste
    lemon juice or vinegar
½ pound "farofa" (toasted manioc flour)

TENDERIZE the round steak with a meat mallet and season with the salt, garlic, black pepper and lemon juice or vinegar. Prepare a "farofa" (see recipe on page 135) with the butter, manioc flour, olives, hardboiled eggs, raisins, scallion and parsley sprig, all chopped fine. Place some of this "farofa" on each slice of round steak, roll and tie (at each end and in the middle) with a thick thread. Heat some lard in a pan, put in the meat rolls and brown on all sides. Add the sauce in which the meat was seasoned to the pan and keep on adding water, a little at a time, until the meat is cooked and tender. Serve in its own gravy.

CALVES KNUCKLES "SINHÁ"

2 calve's knuckles
  salt, garlic, hot peppers, to taste
1 onion
¼ pound lard
  plenty of parsley
1 bay leaf
1 pound peeled tomatoes without seeds
½ cup dry white wine

CUT THE calve's knuckles into medium size pieces and boil in plenty of water with the bay leaf. When well cooked, and the gelatin is thick, heat the lard and sauté the pieces along with the onion, tomatoes, garlic, salt and hot peppers, all finely chopped. Simmer, adding the gelatin little by little. Add the ½ cup dry white wine and mix occasionally in order to avoid having the mixture stick to the bottom of the pan. Continue to cook over a low flame, adding the parsley, chopped fine. Cook for 2 minutes more and serve hot.

"CHURRASCO"
(Rio Grande Barbecue)
beef as desired, preferably fillet or rib steaks

ARRANGE on a spit and insert over brasier at a height to avoid direct flame. Brush occasionally with a mixture of water and salt. Roast to desired preference.

This style of barbecue is from the south, in the state of Rio Grande do Sul, and no seasoning is used. The beef is only brushed with the salted water mixture first on one side until the meat is done and then on the other.

"CHURRASCO PAULISTA"
(São Paulo Barbecue)

tender beef cuts, as desired
lemon juice
lard
salt, garlic and black pepper to taste

SEASON the beef and marinate overnight with salt and lemon juice. The next day, place meat on spit and barbecue over brazier at a suitable level. Brush the meat liberally with lard and turn continuously on the spit so that the meat is well browned on the outside and done medium rare on the inside. Serve with the following sauce:

Barbecue Sauce

vinegar
juice of 1 lemon
plenty of chopped onion
hot peppers

MIX ALL the ingredients together thoroughly and let stand a while before serving. If a milder sauce is desired, add a little water with salt to taste.

COMPLETE "FEIJOADA" CARIOCA
(Black Beans and Meat Rio Style)

2 *pounds black beans*
¾ *pounds pork chops*
¾ *pounds salt pork*
2 *feet, 2 ears and 2 pork tails (optional)*
1 *pound pork sausages, cut in medium size pieces*
2 *smoked (or hot) sausages, cut in medium size pieces*
½ *pound smoked bacon in half slices*
¾ *pound dried beef*
½ *pound lard*
1 *large onion*
3 *tomatoes*
3 *or 4 garlic cloves*
  parsley, scallion, hot peppers and salt to taste
1 *bay leaf*

RINSE the salt pork and the dried beef thoroughly and let soak overnight in plenty of water to remove the excess salt. Soak the black beans in water overnight, too. The next day, drain the beans and place in a large pot with plenty of water and start them cooking. Next, drain the water from the salt pork and dried beef, cover with fresh water in another pot and let boil for a short while. Then remove from heat, drain off the water again and add the meats to the beans after they have been cooking for ½ hour. At this point add the rest of the meats so that they all cook together. Separately, heat the lard and when very hot, sauté the onions and tomatoes (all chopped) and the other condiments. While these are sautéing, taste the "feijoada" and if it requires salt, add the 3 or 4 cloves of garlic, minced and pressed in salt. If the "feijoada" has enough salt, add the minced garlic to the sauté. When this is ready, add a ladle of the cooked beans, mash and mix thoroughly. Then combine with the "feijoada," mixing well, and let simmer on a low flame until all the ingredients are completely cooked and the liquid has thickened. If the liquid thickens too much before all the ingredients are cooked, add *boiling* water as needed. When ready to serve the "feijoada," remove the meats and arrange on a separate platter. The "feijoada" may be served with a ladle from a large tureen.

"Feijoada" is traditionally eaten with rice, "farofa," kale "Mineira" style, hot "feijoada" sauce (see pages 137, 135, 153 and 164, respectively), sliced oranges and a jigger of rum.

FILET MIGNON

> *1 filet mignon*
> *4 tablespoons olive oil*
> *juice of 1 lemon*
> *1 clove garlic pressed in salt*
> *black pepper and hot peppers to taste*
> *scallion and parsley sprig, chopped fine*

CUT THE filet mignon in slices about 1½ inches thick and season with the oil, lemon juice, garlic, salt, black pepper and hot peppers, chopped fine. Let marinate in this sauce for several hours before barbecuing or broiling. When broiling, baste occasionally with the marinating sauce. Serve immediately with rice (see recipe on page 137) and "farofa" (see recipe on page 135).

FLANK STEAK SMOTHERED WITH VEGETABLES

2 pounds flank steak
salt, garlic and hot peppers to taste
onions
lemon juice
1½ pound tomatoes
1 cup dry white wine
some potatoes
carrots
green peppers
½ pound smoked ham or bacon
2 tablespoons butter

CUT FLANK steak into slices and pound with a meat mallet. Wash well and season with the salt, garlic, lemon and hot peppers. Heat the butter in a pot and when melted, remove from flame and add the strips of smoked ham or bacon. Then on top of this add a layer of the flank steak slices, then a layer of carrots in fine slices, then a layer of raw potatoes also cut into fine slices but a little thicker then the carrot slices. Add another layer of flank steak and then a layer of sliced onion and then of green peppers sliced lengthwise. Press down on the mixture to make firm and cover with the tomatoes which have been put through blender with 1 cup of water. Cover the pot, return to heat and cook. When it boils, add salt to taste. When the beef and vegetables are almost tender and the liquid has been almost completely absorbed, add 1 cup dry white wine. Cook a few more minutes. Then remove from heat and serve.

MY OWN "FRITADA"*

8 *eggs*
  salt, black pepper
2 *tablespoons butter*
½ *pound sausage or frankfurters cut in small pieces*
½ *pound ham, chopped*
  parsley sprig
¼ *pound grated cheese*

HEAT the butter. When golden brown, add the pieces of sausage or frankfurters and brown a little. Place in a pyrex baking dish and add the ham chopped in small pieces and spread out evenly. Beat the egg whites until stiff, then add the yolks, grated cheese, salt and a little parsley chopped fine. Mix well and pour over the top. Bake and then serve hot.

"DREAMS OF BRASÍLIA"
(Ham Pancakes)

2 *cups flour*
2½ *cups milk*
3 *eggs yolks*
3 *eggs whites, beaten until stiff*
  salt to taste
1 *tablespoons butter*
½ *pound ham, chopped fine*

---

* See "Glossary for Cooks" on page 247.

COMBINE the flour, milk, egg yolks and salt. Sift and strain so that the ingredients are mixed well and then place in pot. Add the butter and the ham and heat, stirring constantly until mixture lifts easily from the bottom of the pot. (The mixture should be well cooked.) Let cool and then add the egg whites which have been beaten until stiff. Drop batter, by the spoonful, into hot lard and fry.

SÃO PAULO HAM PIE

1 pound flour
2 yeast cakes
1 cup warm milk
4 eggs, beaten
2 tablespoons butter
1 tablespoon lard
1 tablespoon salt
½ teaspoon sugar
1 pound Mozzarella cheese
1 pound ham
1 pound tomatoes
  black pepper, oregano and olive oil to taste
¼ pound grated Parmesan cheese

COMBINE the yeast, sugar and a little flour and dissolve in the warm milk. Let stand for 1 hour. Then add the rest of the ingredients, mix and knead well until the mixture is firm. Grease a deep baking pan. Separate the dough into 2 parts, roll out 1 part and line the bottom of the pan. On top of the dough, spread out half of the Mozzarella cheese and then half of the ham, cut into pieces. Cover this with tomato slices and on top of the tomatoes sprinkle some black pepper, oregano and olive oil. Roll out the second half of the dough and lay this on top of the tomatoes. Then, repeat the one layer of Mozzarella cheese, a layer of ham, a layer of tomatoes, black pepper, oregano and olive oil. Top everything with about ¼ pound of grated Parmesan cheese. Let stand another 20 minutes before baking in a moderate oven for about 40 minutes until golden brown.

HAM PUDDING

½ pound ham, minced
3 tablespoons butter
1 pint milk
½ pound grated Parmesan cheese
4 tablespoons flour
3 eggs
salt and pepper to taste

MAKE a white sauce with the butter, flour, milk, salt and pepper. Mix in the minced ham and grated cheese and then the egg yolks, separately. Finally add in the egg whites, beaten. Mix thoroughly and add salt and pepper as desired. Butter a baking dish, sprinkle with bread crumbs and then pour in the mixture. Use a circular tube pan and place in a tray of hot water. Cook 1 hour, turn out and serve in plate garnished with lettuce, egg slices and cheese strips. Fill the center of the form with mayonnaise.

HAM ROLLS "LAURA"

3 cups flour
2 level tablespoons baking powder
1 teaspoon salt
1 heaping tablespoon butter
2 eggs
1 cup milk
⅔ pounds minced ham mixed with
  2 tablespoons grated Parmesan cheese and
  1 tablespoon butter

SIFT the dry ingredients 3 times then mix in the milk, butter, eggs and knead well. Flour a rolling pin and board and roll out the dough on a cloth napkin dusted with flour. Spread the prepared ham mixture on the dough. With the help of the napkin, roll up the dough with the ham mixture. Let stand 10 minutes. Prepare a buttered baking dish. Cut the roll into medium size slices and arrange in the baking dish. Bake in a hot oven about 20 minutes. When ready, serve with the following sauce:

Wine and Tomato Sauce

2 tablespoons butter or olive oil
1 grated onion
2 cloves pressed garlic
1 pound tomatoes
  salt, black pepper and hot peppers to taste
1 or 2 cups white wine

Place 2 tablespoons butter or olive oil in a frying pan. Heat and add 1 grated onion, 2 cloves of pressed garlic. Sauté and then add 1 pound tomatoes which have been passed through blender. Add salt, hot peppers and black pepper to taste. Then add 1 or 2 cups of white wine and simmer until mixture thickens a little and some of the liquid evaporates.

LIVER "BAIT"

2 pounds liver
2 onions
lard to fry
juice of 2 lemons
salt and pepper to taste

CLEAN liver, cut into small strips and season with salt, pepper and lemon juice. Let stand for 2 hours. Pat in a cloth napkin to remove moisture and fry a little at a time in hot lard. When all the liver strips are fried, cover with 2 onions which have been sliced thin and fried in a little butter. Serve with rice.

LIVER CROQUETTES À LA COPACABANA

1 pound beef liver
1 brain of beef
½ pound chicken liver
1 small grated onion
1 tomato, peeled and seedless
3 egg yolks
1 tablespoon butter
1 tablespoon grated Parmesan cheese
salt, garlic, hot peppers, to taste
bread crumbs
eggs, beaten for breading
oil or lard for frying

WASH the beef liver and brains thoroughly and place in a bowl. Add a little boiling water and cover for a few minutes in order to remove the skin more easily. Then cut into small pieces. Wash the chicken livers in running water and then grind both items together. Heat the butter, salt, garlic, onion and tomato chopped into small pieces. Sauté well, then add the liver mixture and let simmer a little. Add the chopped parsley and peppers. Thicken the mixture with a little flour until it has the desired consistency for croquettes. Remove from heat and let cool a little. Then add the egg yolks. Mix well and place on heat again. Mix well until mixture lifts easily from bottom of pot. Cool and roll into croquettes. Dip in the bread crumbs and then in lightly beaten eggs and then the bread crumbs again. Fry in hot oil or lard.

FRIED OXTAIL

oxtail
onions, chopped
garlic clove, minced
salt, black pepper and minced hot peppers to taste
eggs, beaten
bread crumbs
tomatoes
peas
hearts of palm* (may be omitted)

WASH oxtail thoroughly and cut into sections. Simmer in a sauté of onions, garlic, hot peppers and salt and black pepper to taste. When tender, remove from the gravy, clean off the pieces of seasoning that have stuck and dip sections in bread crumbs, lightly beaten eggs and again the bread crumbs. Fry in lard. When brown, cover with a thick sauce of tomatoes, peas, hearts of palm cut into medium-size pieces sautéed in the oxtail gravy.

---

* See "Glossary for Cooks" on page 247.

OXTAIL STEW FROM SÃO PAULO

2 *pounds oxtail*
2 *tablespoons lard*
1 *chopped onion*
1 *pound tomatoes*
2 *carrots*
1 *scallion and parsley sprig*
1 *tablespoon tomato paste*
   salt and hot peppers to taste
1 *pound potatoes*
3 *green peppers*
2 *cups dry white wine*

WASH the oxtail thoroughly, cut in sections and sauté in lard, with the onion, tomatoes and other condiments. Let brown evenly and then add in the wine and simmer over a low flame. Slowly add in some water, a little at a time, enough to make a little sauce. When oxtail is almost tender, add in diced carrots and potatoes.

Continue to cook over a low flame and stir occasionally to prevent sticking. When ready to serve, remove the meats and vegetables from the gravy and add in the green peppers, sliced lengthwise Serve the oxtail with the gravy.

LOIN OF PORK PUDDING

¾ pound pork loin, ground
¼ pound ham, ground
1 cup bread cubes soaked in milk
2 tablespoons cornstarch dissolved in 1 cup milk
4 egg yolks and 2 egg whites
2 tablespoons bread crumbs
1 tablespoon butter

COMBINE all ingredients. Mix well and bake in greased baking dish, placed in pan of hot water.

"SARAPATEL* DO NORTE"
(Pork Tripe and Giblets Dish from Northern Brazil)

Tripe, giblets and coagulated blood of pork
side of fresh bacon
bay leaf
lemon juice
tomatoes, chopped
onion, chopped
green pepper, chopped
garlic, salt and black pepper to taste
hot peppers, minced
coriander and caraway seeds
vinegar
lard

---

* See "Glossary for Cooks" on page 247.

WASH the tripe and giblets thoroughly in water and lemon juice. Drain and place in boiling, salted water. When water begins to boil again, remove the tripe and giblets and drain. Separately, in plenty of lard, sauté the onion, green pepper, hot peppers, garlic (pressed in salt), tomatoes, all chopped fine, the bay leaf and the side of bacon cut in pieces. Crumble or mince the coagulated blood and season with a little vinegar, black pepper and the coriander and caraway seeds. Combine the blood, tripe and giblets with the sautéed mixture. Simmer well, adding enough water, little by little, to cook the giblets thoroughly. Let simmer until all ingredients are well cooked. When done, this dish should have the consistency of a thick gravy. Serve with rice (see recipe on page 135).

SUCKLING PIG WITH BEER

¼ of a suckling pig
salt to taste
½ pound lard
1 cup beer

SEASON the pork with salt, brush with plenty of lard and wrap in aluminum foil. Place in greased roasting pan in low oven and cook until tender. Then turn the oven up high, remove the foil and continue cooking, basting with the beer, until golden brown.

BAKED SUCKLING PIG WITH ORANGE

1 suckling pig
3 acidic oranges, juiced
1 lemon, juiced
1 onion
   garlic, salt and hot peppers to taste
   scallion and a parsley sprig
2 cups dry white wine
¼ pound lard

CHOOSE a fat young suckling pig about 5 or 6 months old. Wash well and marinate overnight in a sauce made with the condiments, white wine and the orange and lemon juice. Pierce the suckling pig well with a fork beforehand so that the marinating sauce penetrates it. The next day grease the piglet on the outside and place in a lightly greased roasting pan. Roast in a medium oven so that it cooks slowly. Turn the piglet occasionally and baste with the marinating sauce. Serve with "farofa" and rice (see pages 135 and 137).

SAUSAGE OR FRANKFURTER SURPRISE

14 tablespoons flour
3 tablespoons lard
2 egg yolks and 1 egg white
1 tablespoon baking powder
1 tablespoon sugar
   milk enough to form a batter
   sausage or frankfurters in quantity desired

103

Sift flour, baking powder, sugar and salt. Add in the yolks, un-beaten and the egg whites. Add in the lard and enough milk to form a soft batter. Knead, roll out and cut in narrow strips. Place a piece of sausage or frankfurter in the center of each strip and roll. Brush each "surprise" with egg yolks and bake in hot oven.

SÃO PAULO STEW

1 pound stew beef
2 onions
1 pound tomatoes
4 cloves garlic pressed in salt
  black pepper and hot peppers to taste
  bay leaf and parsley sprig
½ pound lard
  The following ingredients in the quantities desired
  and cut in medium size pieces:
  pork chops
  sausages
  smoked pork
  bacon
  potatoes
  sweet potatoes
  manioc or yucca if available
  turnips
  pumpkin
  cabbage
  kale leaves
  plantains (cooking bananas)

HEAT the lard in a pot and when very hot, add the pieces of stew beef. Let fry, turning the pieces continuously so that the meat browns evenly on all sides. Add a little water and let simmer. When the meat is tender, add the onions, sliced, the tomatoes, hot peppers, black pepper, garlic, parsley and bay leaf. Add plenty of water and let boil long enough to make a rich broth, adding salt to taste. An hour before serving, add the pieces of pork chops, sausages, smoked pork and bacon as well as the potatoes, sweet potatoes, manioc and turnips. Let boil, and when these ingredients are cooked, a short while before serving, add the pumpkin, cabbage, shredded kale leaves and plantains. When these last added ingredients are cooked, the stew is ready. Serve with the following sauce:

São Paulo Stew Sauce

lard
onion
tomatoes, sliced
garlic pressed in salt
carrots
green peppers, cut in lengthwise strips
black pepper and hot peppers to taste

HEAT a little lard and when very hot add the onion, chopped, the sliced tomatoes and the garlic and salt. When brown, add finely chopped carrots and plenty of green pepper strips along with the black pepper and hot peppers, minced. Add a little water to this mixture and boil until the sauce thickens. When ready to serve the São Paulo stew, arrange the meats in the middle of a large platter, surrounded by the vegetables, and cover with this sauce. Serve hot together with "pirão" (see the recipe below). The sauce may also be served separately in a gravy bowl.

"Pirão"

This "pirão" is a type of "mush" made with manioc flour* and the thick broth in which the meat and vegetables of the São Paulo stew were cooked. The thick broth or gravy should be heated and enough manioc flour should be slowly added to give the desired consistency. The "pirão" should be stirred constantly to avoid lumping.

The "pirão" is a common "side dish" in Brazil and can be made using the liquid from any dish —as for example, fish, shrimp, chicken or other meat dishes— giving off a broth or gravy.

---

* See "Glossary for Cooks" on page 247.

POULTRY DISHES

POULTRY DISHES

CHICKEN BRAZILIAN STYLE

1 frying chicken
salt and pepper to taste
hot peppers
1 onion, sliced
5 tablespoons butter
1 pint cream, beaten without sugar
2 cups chicken broth
1 can peas
½ pound fresh asparagus tips
½ pound fresh cauliflower
5 tomatoes, peeled, without seeds

HAVE the chicken cut in parts and rinse in water and lemon juice, then dry. Sprinkle with salt and pepper, brown in butter and then place in a roaster with the same butter in which chicken was sautéed, together with the asparagus tips, cauliflower, onion, tomatoes and whipped cream. Cover and roast until all ingredients are cooked and chicken is tender. Serve with chicken gravy (see recipe on the following page).

Chicken Gravy

2 cups chicken broth
chicken giblets
condiments as desired
3 egg yolks
1 tablespoon butter
2 tablespoons flour
milk as needed

COOK the giblets in 8 cups water together with the chicken broth and condiments desired. When done, strain. There should be 4 cups of liquid obtained. If not, add milk. Into the gravy, mix the egg yolks, 1 tablespoon butter and the flour. Heat until cooked and mixture thickens. When the chicken and the vegetables are done, place on pyrex plate and cover with the gravy. Return to oven for a few minutes. Serve hot.

CHICKEN WITH APPLES

1 frying chicken
2 apples
¼ pound lard
1 onion
3 tomatoes
parsley, garlic, salt and hot peppers to taste

HEAT the lard and sauté the onion, chopped tomatoes, salt and pressed garlic, hot peppers and parsley, all chopped. When brown, add the chicken cut in parts and let it brown a little. Then add a little water, a little at a time, in order to cook the chicken and make some broth (about 3 cups). After it is cooked, remove from flame and shred the meat, discarding the bones. Separately, prepare the chicken sauce below.

Next, peel the apples and slice thin into a bowl with water and lemon so that the slices do not turn brown. Using a deep pyrex baking dish, pour in one layer of the sauce, follow with one layer of apple slices, then the chicken. Keep repeating, ending with a top layer of sauce. Sprinkle with grated cheese and butter chips. Bake until golden brown and serve.

Chicken Sauce

> *4 tablespoons flour*
> *1½ cups milk*
> *3 cups chicken broth*
> *10 tablespoons grated Parmesan cheese*
> *4 eggs*
> *2 tablespoons butter*

STRAIN the chicken broth and pour into a pot with butter, egg yolks and flour which has been slowly dissolved in the milk. Add salt and black pepper to taste. Stir constantly until the mixture thickens and is cooked. Then, add the grated cheese, mix well and leave for 5 more minutes over the flame, then remove.

BAKED CHICKEN AND RICE

1 *frying chicken*
½ *pound butter*
¼ *pound lard*
8 *peeled tomatoes without seeds*
   salt, black pepper, and garlic to taste
   dry white wine or vinegar
3 *tablespoons grated cheese*
1 *pound rice*
1 *bay leaf*
2 *sweet red peppers*
   small dill pickles, chopped
¼ *pound olives*
1 *can peas*
2 *hardboiled eggs*
3 *egg yolks*

MARINATE the chicken overnight in a sauce of dry white wine or vinegar and garlic pressed in salt. The next day, heat ¼ pound butter and add 1 onion, chopped. Let brown a little and then add the tomatoes, chopped, and the chicken, cut into parts. Simmer a little and then slowly add in the marinating sauce and water, little by little, until the chicken is tender. Prepare the rice, using lard and onion (as in the recipe on page 137), and cook completely until water has evaporated and rice grains are loose and separate. Butter a large baking pan and garnish with slices of sweet red pepper cut lengthwise and slices of pickles. Then line the bottom of the pan with some of the rice. Combine with the remaining rice, the other ¼ pound butter, the 3 egg yolks, beaten, the grated

Parmesan cheese, and the chicken, which has been boned, the olives, chopped, and the can of peas which have been rinsed in hot water and drained previously. Also add in the sauce (strained) in which the chicken was cooked and the hardboiled eggs, chopped. Mix well and press into baking pan. Sprinkle bread crumbs and butter chips on top, and then bake in a medium over for 20 minutes. When ready to serve, turn out and garnish with lettuce leaves, tomato slices, olives, etc.

CHICKEN WITH CORN

kernels from 10 ears of corn or 2 cans of corn
1 frying chicken
1 pound tomatoes
1 onion
¼ pound lard
¼ pound butter
1 bay leaf
salt, pepper, garlic, hot peppers, scallions
and parsley, to taste

CUT CHICKEN in parts, wash and season with lemon juice, salt, garlic. lemon and hot peppers. Combine the butter and lard and heat. When very hot add the chicken parts and brown evenly. Add the onion, tomatoes and bay leaf. Let simmer and then add the corn. (If using canned corn, do not add corn until chicken is almost done.) Keep adding enough water to cook the chicken and corn thoroughly and make a sauce. When ready to serve, remove from flame and add the scallion, parsley and onion, chopped fine. Serve hot with rice (see recipe on page 137).

113

MY FAVORITE CHICKEN

1 large frying chicken
¼ pound lard
1 onion
tomatoes
garlic, salt and hot peppers to taste
1 cup dry white wine
lemon juice

CUT CHICKEN in parts and season with salt, garlic and lemon juice. Heat the lard and sauté the onion, tomatoes, garlic and hot peppers. Add the chicken parts and simmer. Add the white wine and some water, a little at a time, to cook the chicken. When the chicken is browned and cooked, remove from heat and let cool slightly. Remove the bones and arrange in a pyrex baking dish covered with the chicken sauce below. Bake in a moderate oven until golden.

Chicken Sauce with Cream Cheese

3 cups milk
¾ pounds cream cheese
2 tablespoons butter
4 egg yolks
2 tablespoons cornstarch or flour

COMBINE the cheese, 2 cups of milk, 2 tablespoons butter and a little salt in a pot and heat, stirring constantly until it reaches the boiling point. Then add the remaining cup of milk into which the 4 egg yolks and the flour have been well blended. Continue stirring constantly until mixture thickens. Cover the chicken with this sauce.

CHICKEN IN MY OWN STYLE

2 *roasting chickens*
1 *pound tomatoes*
2 *onions, small*
¼ *pound butter*
1 *cup ketchup*
3 *tablespoons mustard*
   salt, black pepper, garlic, lemon juice,
   vinegar and oil to taste
1 *hot pepper*
½ *teaspoon paprika*
1 *wine glass dry wine*
½ *pint fresh unsweetened cream, whipped*
½ *cup milk*
1 *tablespoon flour*
½ *pound cream cheese*
1 *can mushrooms*

MARINATE the chickens overnight with salt, garlic, lemon juice, vinegar, black pepper and oil. The next day, roast the chickens, adding water as needed and cook until tender. Let brown, then remove from heat and strain the remaining liquid, removing some of the fat. There should be about 2 cups of liquid left. Slice the breast meat of the chickens into thin slices. After removing the bones and discarding the skin, cut the rest of the chicken meat with poultry scissors into small thin strips. Heat the butter and when golden brown, add the tomatoes and onions which have been blended and strained. Let simmer a little and then add in the dark meat of the chickens, the paprika, hot pepper, mustard, the liquid

115

in which the chickens cooked, the mushrooms chopped fine, the wine and simmer. Then add in the pieces of cream cheese, and stir until well blended. Then add in the cream, salt to taste and continue stirring until mixture has the consistency of a thick cream sauce. If necessary, add in the flour dissolved in milk to thicken the mixture. Serve hot over the slices of chicken breast with applesause and pieces of pear cooked in red wine.

SÃO PAULO ANNIVERSARY CHICKEN*

1 large frying chicken
¼ pound butter
¼ pound lard
4 eggs
1 pound bread crumbs
onion
scallion and parsley sprig
2 cups dry white wine
juice of 1 acidic orange
juice of 1 lemon
salt and black pepper to taste
hot peppers, minced
1 bay leaf

CLEAN the chicken, cut into parts and marinate overnight in a sauce made with the wine, juice of orange and lemon and the condiments. The next day, heat the butter and lard. Add the bay

---

* This recipe was made in honor of the 400th anniversary of the founding of São Paulo which was celebrated in 1954. The celebration lasted the entire year with exhibits, shows, etc.

leaf and chicken and let brown over a low flame. Keep basting with the marinating sauce and simmer until the chicken is tender. Then remove from heat, strain the liquid and dip the chicken parts in bread crumbs, then in lightly beaten eggs and then in the bread crumbs. Fry in hot lard. Serve with bananas dipped in beaten eggs and bread crumbs and then fried in lard; slices of pineapple fried in butter; pears cooked in red wine; bacon strips fried in lard and slices of ham.

Next, arrange the pieces of chicken in the center of a large platter and surround with the fruits, bacon and ham. Cover with the following sauce:

Anniversary Sauce

HEAT ½ pound butter and when golden brown, add 2 sliced onions; 1 pound tomatoes, blended and strained; salt, garlic and hot peppers to taste. When the sauce is thick, add in 1½ quarts of unsweetened whipped cream. Boil a little more, until thickened and pour over chicken.

SMOKED COUNTRY STYLE CHICKEN

1 frying chicken
onion
garlic, salt, black pepper and hot peppers to taste
vinegar
butter
lemon juice
1 green pepper, chopped
bacon
lard

Overnight, season the chicken with the condiments. The next day, remove the condiments and brush the chicken thoroughly, inside and outside, with butter. Wrap the chicken with bacon strips, tying the strips in place with string. Place chopped green pepper and 1 onion inside the chicken for taste. Wrap the chicken in aluminum foil and place in greased roasting pan. Roast in moderate oven until tender. Remove and cut chicken in parts. With the drippings from the roasting pan, make the following sauce:

Chicken Sauce

chicken drippings
2 cups milk
3 egg yolks
4 tablespoons grated cheese
2 level tablespoons flour
canned peas

Combine ingredients and heat until mixture thickens, stirring constantly. Arrange the chicken on a platter and cover with the sauce. Sprinkle the grated cheese and the canned peas (warmed and drained) on top.

CHICKEN "VATAPÁ"*

*¾ pounds rice flour or flour
milk from 1 coconut
1 pound tomatoes
dendê oil or olive oil
1 young spring chicken
condiments as desired*

SAUTÉ the tomatoes and condiments. Cut the chicken in parts and brown. Then add a little water and simmer until cooked. When the chicken is ready, remove the bones, pour the gravy into a pot and thicken with the rice flour or flour, while stirring constantly over a low flame. (The flour should be added slowly so as to avoid making the mixture too thick.) When the mixture has thickened, add the chicken and let simmer a little while longer. When ready to remove from heat, add the coconut milk† and the dendê or olive oil as desired. Serve with rice flour "angú" (see recipe on page 139).

---

* See "Glossary for Cooks" on page 247.
† See recipe on page 173.

DUCK WITH ORANGE

1 *medium size duck*
1 *onion*
  garlic pressed in salt
  salt, black pepper and hot peppers to taste
1 *clove*
1 *sprig mint*
  scallion and parsley sprig
1 *cup olive oil*
1 *quart water*
2 *cups vinegar*
2 *cups white wine*
1 *cup lemon juice*
2 *cups orange juice*

BLEND the onion, garlic, salt, black pepper, hot peppers, clove, mint, scallion, parsley sprig and olive oil in a blender or put through a meat grinder. Rub the duck thoroughly, inside and outside, with this mixture of condiments and let stand for 3 hours. Then place the duck in a deep dish and add the water, vinegar, white wine, lemon juice and orange juice and let marinate overnight. Turn often while marinating, but allow the duck to remain with its breast down in the marinating sauce the greater part of the time. On the following day, drain the duck, dry thoroughly and then rub with butter and lard, inside and out. Roast in a moderate oven, basting frequently with the marinating sauce, until the duck is tender and golden brown. Serve garnished with slices of orange.

DUCK WITH TUCUPÍ SAUCE
(Specialty of Pará)

1 duck
lard
butter
salt, black pepper and hot chili pepper to taste
garlic pressed in salt
vinegar and lemon juice
tucupí sauce
"jambú" leaves

MARINATE the duck overnight with a sauce made from the salt, black pepper, hot chili pepper, garlic, vinegar and lemon juice. The next day, dry the duck well and brush with plenty of lard and butter inside and outside. Grease a roasting pan, place the duck in it, wrapped in aluminum foil, and add the marinating sauce. Roast in a moderate oven, basting occasionally with the marinating sauce, until the meat is tender. When the duck is done, remove the aluminum foil and let stay in the oven a few minutes more until golden brown. When ready, take the duck out of the oven, let cool and then cut into parts at the joints. Next arrange the pieces of roasted duck in a pot, add a few "jambú" leaves* and cover with tucupí sauce (see recipe on page 167). Place over a low

---

* "Jambú" is an herb which is native to Pará in the north of Brazil, where it is used to season only certain dishes—mostly those served with tucupí sauce. The herb has a round leaf and is very pungent. Since, apparently, "jambú" is solely found in Pará and the other parts of the Amazon region of Brazil, any other pungent herb may be substituted in its place.

121

fire and let simmer for half an hour. If the tucupí sauce dries up, add a little water so that there is some sauce remaining when the duck is ready. Add some hot chili peppers (to taste). When ready to serve, remove the "jambú" leaves.

STUFFED TURKEY WITH ORANGE BRAZILIAN STYLE

CLEAN and wash turkey and marinate overnight in the following mixture:

Press some cloves of garlic with salt and combine with 2 onions, 1 clove, parsley and scallion, 1 bay leaf, 1 sprig mint, hot pepper, black pepper and 1 cup oil. Put mixture through meat grinder or blender. Rub fowl thoroughly with the mixture, inside and outside and let stand for 3 hours. Then place in a deep dish adding 3 quarts of water, 1 quart vinegar, 1 quart white wine, 1 cup lemon juice and 2 cups orange juice. Turn frequently while marinating, but preferably allowing the turkey to remain breast down the greater part of the time. (The orange juice gives the turkey a very special taste. It should always be seasoned the day before it is to be cooked.)

Stuffing for the Gullet, Rio Grande Style:

COOK the turkey giblets and when ready, chop fine. In butter, sauté an onion, garlic, hot peppers, scallion and parsley sprig, all chopped fine. Add the chopped giblets, ½ pound seedless raisins, 3 hard-boiled eggs, chopped fine, ½ pound chopped, pitted olives and

122

some bread slices, broken in pieces. Mix all the ingredients thoroughly and use to stuff the gullet.

"Farofa" Stuffing for the Body

SAUTÉ 1 finely chopped onion and 4 peeled tomatoes (remove seeds) in 4 tablespoons butter. Combine with chopped ham, olives (pitted), 1 pound manioc flour,* chopped boiled eggs, salt to taste and chopped parsley. This mixture should remain moist.

Stuffing with Chestnuts, Raisins and Prunes

SLIT and roast 2 pounds chestnuts, then peel and grind. Heat 3 tablespoons butter and add in the ground chestnuts, mixing constantly using 2 forks to keep mixture separated. Add ½ pound seedless raisins, ½ pound chopped black prunes, ⅔ pound manioc flour and mix continuously until lightly browned. Remove from flame and stuff.

How to Roast the Turkey

PLACE the stuffed turkey in a roasting pan and grease well with butter and melted lard. Take two large clean dish towels or pieces of cheese cloth, moisten in the sauce used to marinate the turkey and thoroughly brush with butter or lard. Cover the gullet and breast of the turkey with these towels and fasten under the wings. Then wrap the turkey completely in aluminum foil or in a large

---

* See "Glossary for Cooks" on page 247.

123

cloth prepared as previously described. Pour two cups of the marinating sauce in the bottom of the roasting pan and place in a hot oven. While roasting, baste the turkey occasionally with the marinating sauce. When the turkey is tender, remove the aluminum foil, to brown the turkey. Turn the turkey on all sides so that it brown evenly, making sure to baste it often with the marinating sauce and drippings from the roasting pan.

BEAN DISHES

"Beans for breakfast, beans for lunch, and hot baked beans for tea..."

Beans, alas, have fallen into disrepute with most Americans —a disrepute which was probably acquired during the war days when beans were, in fact, standard army-navy fare for breakfast, lunch and tea. The blame, however, shouldn't be laid to the beans or the repetitiousness of the fare but rather to the type of "cooks" impressed into kitchen duty in the armed forces.

Brazilians —figuratively speaking— also serve beans for breakfast, lunch and tea, but unlike the G.I. Joe, they look forward to it. Should Mrs. Brazilian housewife serve a meal sans beans, the wrath of her lord and master is sure to rain on her head.

This Brazilian passion for beans may be because Brazil is the world's greatest producer of beans and Brazilians out of sheer patriotism feel they must support the native industry. It's more likely, though, that the Brazilians are just naturally better cooks who just naturally know how to turn out superlative bean dishes —as the following recipes will bear out.

.... BEAN DISHES ....

HOME STYLE BEANS

1 pound beans (Brazilian usually prefer the black beans,
but any kind may be used)
1 thick slice salt pork
ham bone (optional)
1 hot sausage
2 tablespoons olive oil or pork lard
2 cloves garlic, minced
1 onion, chopped
salt, black pepper and hot peppers to taste

SOAK the beans and the salt pork (separately) overnight. The next day, drain the beans and pork, and cook them in a pot with the ham bone and enough salted water to cover. While the beans are cooking, sauté the hot sausage, chopped, and the garlic, black pepper and hot peppers, minced, in the olive oil. When the beans are boiling and the sauté is ready, add the sauté to the beans. Mix well, cover and let simmer until the beans are tender. Before the beans have cooked, test for seasoning and correct if necessary. When ready to serve, remove the ham bone.

"ACARAJÉ"
(Navy Bean Purée with Shrimp Sauce)

4 tablespoons dendê oil (or substitute olive oil)
1 pound navy beans
1 tablespoon salt
1 onion
1 clove garlic

SOAK beans overnight. The next day, shell, cut off black ends and put through meat grinder, using flat blade, together with onion and garlic. Salt to taste. Mix in blender until mixture whitens. Using a tablespoon, spoon mixture into hot oil and fry. Serve with shrimp sauce below.

Shrimp Sauce

1 cup dried shrimp
1 cup dendê oil (or substitute olive oil)
1 onion
1 tablespoon cayenne pepper

PUT DRY ingredients through meat grinder. Heat the oil in frying pan then add in the puréed ingredients, stirring continuously to prevent drying out. Serve cold.

COCONUT NAVY BEANS NORTHERN STYLE

1 pound navy beans
  milk of 1 large coconut
1 onion
  garlic pressed in salt
3 tomatoes
1 green pepper
  coriander seeds

COOK the navy beans in boiling, salted water with all the condiments chopped fine. When almost all the water has evaporated, put the cooked beans through a strainer so as to make a purée. Return to pot and add in the coconut milk (see recipe on page 171). Stir constantly until mixture boils and thickens. Remove from heat and serve immediately.

"TUTÚ"* OF BLACK BEANS

1 pound cooked black beans
¼ pound lard
½ pound fried bacon rind
  bacon strips
½ pound sausages, fried
  onion, garlic, hot peppers and salt, to taste
½ pound manioc flour†

---

* "Tutú" is a dish made with cooked black beans (usually "leftovers") which have been puréed or liquefied and then re-cooked with manioc flour and other ingredients (as desired) to form a firm, but not hard, mass.
† See "Glossary for Cooks" on page 247.

129

Heat the lard and sauté the onion, garlic, hot peppers and salt.
Fry the sausages, mince them and add to the sautéed mixture.
Simmer lightly. Meanwhile pass the cooked beans (with plenty of
sauce) through a strainer or blender. Then add to the sautéed
mixture and let boil. Add the bacon rind and sprinkle in the
manioc flour slowly, mixing constantly until a paste is formed.
This "tutú" is served with fried bacon strips arranged around the
plate, Kale "Mineira" (see recipe on page 153) and fried eggs.

"TUTÚ OU VIRADO PAULISTA"
(São Paulo "Tutú")

1 pound kidney beans or other dried beans
1 minced onion
hot peppers
1 bay leaf
pressed garlic
parsley sprig
1 scallion
salt and pepper to taste
¼ pound pork lard
¼ pound smoked bacon, whole
½ pound fried bacon rind
½ pound manioc flour
1 pound pork sausages, fried
fried eggs, as desired

Soak the beans and smoked bacon overnight. Cook in plenty of
water until tender. (When cooked, there should be plenty of sauce

remaining.) While beans are still cooking add a little salt. Sauté
the onion, garlic and salt to taste. When evenly browned, add the
beans and sauce and simmer. When mixture has thickened, sprinkle
in the manioc flour* slowly, mixing constantly, until a smooth paste
is formed. It should be firm but not hard. Add the bacon rind,
well minced, and the peppers, scallion and parsley, chopped fine.
Mix a little and remove from heat. To serve, arrange in a platter,
surrounded with fried pork sausages and the fried eggs. Serve hot
with rice (see recipe on page 137).

---

* See "Glossary for Cooks" on page 247.

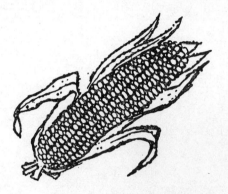

GRAIN and CEREAL DISHES

SECTION EIGHT

──────────GRAIN and CEREAL DISHES──────────

"FAROFA"
(Toasted Manioc Flour*)

½ pound butter
1 pound manioc flour
½ onion, chopped
salt to taste

HEAT the butter in a large frying pan. Add the chopped onion and brown lightly. Then add the salt and manioc flour, stirring constantly until mixture is golden brown and is crumbly.

In place of onion, finely diced Portuguese sausage or chopped hard-boiled egg may be substituted according to taste. Brazilians mix "farofa" with any and all dishes or eat it simply by itself.

──────────

* If manioc flour is not available in your grocery or supermarket, farina may be substituted in its place.

CARROT "FAROFA"

4 carrots, grated
3 eggs, beaten
1 onion, chopped
1 tablespoon lard
parsley
2 tablespoon butter
½ pound manioc flour, toasted
salt to taste

HEAT 1 tablespoon butter, pour in beaten eggs and scramble so that they are in small pieces. Remove from stove and place in plate. Heat the lard and other tablespoon butter. Add in the parsley, chopped onion and grated carrots. Mix thoroughly and then add in the eggs and lastly, the toasted manioc flour (see recipe on page 135). Mix well and serve hot with any meat dishes.

CORN "FAROFA"

kernels from 5 ears corn or 1 can corn
2 tablespoon butter
1 onion
3 tomatoes, peeled, without seeds
parsley sprig
garlic, salt and hot pepper to taste
"farofa" (toasted manioc flour), as needed

HEAT the butter and sauté condiments, all finely chopped. When brown, add in the corn and simmer a little, slowly, adding sufficient water, a little at a time, so that the corn cooks thoroughly. When the water has almost evaporated and the corn is tender, add a little more butter and mix in a little toasted manioc flour (see recipe on page 135) or toasted corn flour. The mixture should be crumbly and fluffy. The quantity of corn should be greater than the flour used.

RICE BRAZILIAN STYLE

1 pound rice
1 onion, minced
2 cloves garlic pressed in salt
2 tablespoons lard

Wash and drain off the rice. Heat the lard and when very hot add in the minced onion, salt and garlic. Tomatoes and tomato paste may also be added if desired. Sauté the mixture then add in the rice. Stir continuously until the rice has cooked a little and is browned lightly. Then, add hot water (2 cups of water to each cup of rice) or until rice is covered by about 1¼ inches. Cover and when water boils vigorously, diminish the flame letting the rice continue simmering over a very low flame until all the water has evaporated and rice is tender with each grain separated.

BAKED RICE "JAÚ"

3 cups rice
lard or oil
garlic pressed with salt
1 chopped onion
scallion and parsley sprig
½ pound grated Parmesan cheese
½ pound ham
¼ pound olives
¼ pound butter
4 tablespoons bread crumbs
3 eggs, beaten
3 eggs, hardboiled and sliced

PREPARE the rice as indicated on page 137. When ready and still warm, mix in the 3 beaten eggs. Arrange the rice in layers in a casserole. Between the layers of rice spread the slices of ham, hardboiled eggs, olives, grated cheese and pieces of butter. The top layer should be of rice. Sprinkle grated cheese, bread crumbs and butter chips on top. Garnish with olives and slices of boiled eggs and tomatoes. Bake for ½ hour in a moderate oven and serve hot.

COCONUT RICE

1 pound rice
milk of 1 large coconut
salt to taste

WASH and drain the rice and then boil in salted water. When cooked, add in the coconut milk (see recipe on page 173) and mash until mixture becomes a consistent paste. Place in a buttered mold and place mold in tray of hot water so that rice remains hot until served. Turn out and serve with "efó," "vatapá" (see recipes on pages 74 and 75) and other dishes from Bahia.

RICE FLOUR "ANGÚ"*

¾ *pounds rice flour*
2 *tablespoons butter*
scallion and parsley sprig
salt to taste

Cook the scallion and parsley in about 1 quart of water, slightly salted. When the water is boiling, remove the scallion and parsley, add the 2 tablespoons butter and then the rice flour which has been previously dissolved in a little cold water. Stir constantly until the mixture thickens and takes on the consistency of a very heavy sauce, almost like a soft purée. Pour the "angú" into a pan or mold and let cool. When ready to serve, cut into slices and serve along with "vatapá" (see recipe on page 75).

---

* *Angú* is a type of "mush" usually made by cooking corn meal in boiling water, salted to taste. It can be cooked until it is of a thick (but not firm) consistency. In these cases, it is generally spooned out hot and served as an accompaniment to meat or poultry dishes. It may also be cooked somewhat longer so that it becomes firm when allowed to cool. In these cases, it is commonly sliced and served cold.

CHEESE
and MACARONI DISHES

SECTION NINE

━━━━━━CHEESE and MACARONI DISHES━━━━━━

BREAD AND CHEESE OMELETTE

5 *eggs*
½ *cup milk*
1 *cup of bread cubes*
¼ *pound grated cheese*
salt to taste
chopped parsley

TRIM 1 loaf of bread and cube the inner portion enough to fill 1 cup. Mix the bread cubes and milk in blender then add in the egg yolks, grated cheese and salt. Remove from blender and add in the egg whites beaten until stiff. Heat 1 tablespoon butter in a frying pan and when hot, pour the mixture evenly in the pan. Cook over a low flame and keep stirring lightly with a fork so that the omelette remains fluffy and light and with some lumps. Just before removing from flame sprinkle a little of the chopped parsley on top.

BAKED MACARONI BRAZILIAN STYLE

1 *pound macaroni*
3 *tablespoons butter*
½ *pound ham*
½ *pound Mozzarella cheese*
¼ *pound grated Parmesan cheese*
½ *pound beef, ground*
  onion, tomatoes, garlic, salt and other condiments
  as desired

PREPARE a meat sauce using the ground beef and a sauté of chopped onion, garlic, peeled tomatoes without seeds and other condiments as desired. Cook the macaroni in boiling, salted water. When done, drain, and while still hot, mix in some butter chips. Then add the meat and tomato sauce and mix thoroughly. Arrange in layers in a baking dish, alternating with the mozzarella cheese and strips of ham. The top layer should be of macaroni. Sprinkle grated Parmesan cheese on top and bake in a hot oven until brown. When the grated cheese has melted, remove from oven and serve.

"MINEIRINHOS"
(Cheese and Olive Muffins from Minas)

2 cups grated cheese
½ cup chopped green olives
½ cup milk
1 tablespoon butter
2 whole eggs
pinch of salt
1 level teaspoon flour

BEAT the eggs. Add the salt, cheese, flour, olives, milk and butter. Mix well and pour into buttered muffin tins. Bake in a moderate oven until golden brown. Serve with meat dishes.

VEGETABLE DISHES

VEGETABLE DISHES

RED CABBAGE

1 medium size red cabbage, shredded
¼ pound side of bacon,
  chopped into medium size pieces
2 green apples
1 clove
  salt to taste

Fᴿʏ ᴛʜᴇ bacon pieces, add the shredded cabbage, a little salt, the clove and the apples, peeled and quartered. Cover and steam over a very low flame. Serve with parsley potatoes and pork chops.

SALTY "CANJICA" CAKE
(Corn Cake)

1 pound dried, white corn kernels
3 eggs
3 tablespoons flour
2 tablespoons butter, melted
1½ cups milk
  salt and pepper to taste
  chopped parsley sprig

SOAK the corn kernels in water overnight. Boil in salted water. When cooked, drain and combine in a blender (or put through a meat grinder or strainer) with the milk. Then add the flour, egg yolks and melted butter and blend for a few minutes. Pour into buttered pyrex baking dish and add the egg whites (beaten until stiff) and the parsley. Mix lightly then place in hot oven to bake. Do not brown very much. This dish is specially good with pork but may be served with any meat dish.

CORN CROQUETTES

> *kernels from 10 ears of corn or 2 cans of corn*
> *1½ cups milk*
> *1 onion*
> *3 tomatoes*
> *hot peppers*
> *salt and garlic*
> *1 tablespoon butter*
> *4 tablespoons flour*
> *bread crumbs*
> *4 eggs*
> *lard or oil to fry*

HEAT the butter and add finely chopped onion, peppers, garlic and salt to taste. Add the kernels of corn and sauté. Then add enough water to cook thoroughly. When the corn is cooked and water almost evaporated, take out 1 cupful of the corn and put aside. Place the milk, 2 egg yolks, 4 tablespoons flour in liquefier and blend well. Then pour in the corn mixture and again mix well. Place the mixture in a pot adding the 1 cupful of corn which was put aside earlier, and heat until it thickens. Stir constantly to avoid lumps. If mixture is not firm enough, add a little flour to give more consistency. When mixture can be lifted easily from the bottom of the pot, it is ready. Remove from heat and let cook. Then form into croquettes. Dip the croquettes in the bread crumbs, then in lightly beaten eggs (2) and again in the bread crumbs. Fry in lard or oil until golden brown. Remove with pancake turner and place on absorbent paper to take up excess fat.

HEARTS OF PALM* SALAD

1 can hearts of palm
2 onions
3 tomatoes
4 hardboiled eggs
   green olives
   scallions
   your favorite dressing or vinegar, oil, salt, pepper, and minced garlic and parsley, mixed well.

Arrange platter with onions, scallions, tomatoes, pitted olives, hard-boiled eggs and finally the hearts of palm, all sliced. Pour the dressing over all.

---

* Hearts of palm, or "palmito," as they are called in Brazil, consist of the tender terminal bud of the palm tree, before it shoots out of the stem. Several kinds of palm may be used, such as the coconut palm. Hearts of palm resemble canned asparagus and artichoke hearts somewhat in taste and texture. This delicate vegetable, canned and exported from Brazil, is becoming more and more popular with Americans. It is available in some of the larger food markets and shops specializing in imported delicacies.

HEARTS OF PALM* OMELETTE

1 can hearts of palm
5 eggs
 grated Parmesan cheese
 salt, black pepper and hot peppers to taste
1 onion
1 tomato

SAUTÉ the hot peppers, onion and tomato, all chopped fine, in one tablespoon of either lard, butter or olive oil. After these ingredients are cooked together, add the hearts of palm (do not overcook them). When ready, arrange the hearts in a pyrex dish which should be greased with butter. Beat eggs (white first and then yolks) and pour over the hearts of palm. Sprinkle the surface of the omelette with grated cheese and bake in oven (350° F) until golden.

HEARTS OF PALM* PARMIGIANA OR MILANESE

1 can hearts of palm
3 eggs
 bread crumbs
 salt, black pepper and hot peppers to taste
 lard
 Mozzarella or American cheese sliced

SLICE the hearts of palm in lengthwise strips. Dip the slices in beaten eggs (seasoned), then bread crumbs and then again in the eggs.

---

* See "Glossary for Cooks" on page 247.

Deep-fry the slices. Next, arrange the slices in a pyrex dish and place the cheese slices on top, allowing them to melt in oven (350° F).

Note: To prepare the milanese recipe, proceed exactly as above but eliminate the cheese.

KALE "MINEIRA" STYLE

2 bundles tender young kale
1 small onion
  garlic pressed in salt
  lard

HEAT the lard and sauté the onion, cut in thin slices, and the pressed garlic. Then add in the kale, shredded. Let sauté for only a few minutes so that the kale becomes tender but does not lose its color. Serve immediately.

CREAMED POTATOES

1 pound potatoes cooked with salt
½ pound butter
½ cup cream
5 eggs, separated
1 tablespoon grated Parmesan cheese
  salt, black pepper and other condiments to taste

BOIL, peel and mash the potatoes. Add the cream, little by little, stirring constantly. Then add the butter which has been melted in a double boiler. Next, add the egg yolks. Beat well and then add the egg whites, beaten stiff. Bake in a hot oven in a greased baking dish and serve hot.

"NHOQUE"
(Potato Fritters, Brazilian Style)

1 pound potatoes
1 heaping tablespoon flour
½ tablespoon butter
4 tablespoons grated Parmesan cheese
1 egg
salt to taste

BOIL the potatoes in a little salted water. When done, mash and place in a bowl, adding in the flour, butter, unbeaten egg and cheese. Mix well. Flour hands and board and pat mixture into rolls. Slice into medium size pieces and fry the "nhoques," a few at a time in hot lard. Sprinkle with a mixture of grated cheese, 1 raw carrot, grated, salt and pepper to taste. Serve hot.

QUICK APPLE PUDDING FOR MEAT DISHES

4 apples
4 tablespoons sugar
3 whole eggs
2 tablespoons flour
5 tablespoons milk
lemon juice

PEEL and cut apples into fine slices. Add a little lemon juice, and powdered sugar and mash with two forks or finger tips. Then add the milk, flour and beaten eggs. Mix well and pour in a buttered baking dish set in a pan of water. Bake in medium oven.

TRICOLOR PUDDING

4 cups milk
4 large raw carrots, grated
½ pound dried peas
1 pound potatoes
3 egg yolks
½ pound butter
¼ pound olives and
¼ pound tomatoes, sliced
⅓ pound grated Parmesan cheese
4 heaping tablespoons cornstarch

SOAK the peas in water for a few hours. Then cook in little water until done and almost all of the water has evaporated. Remove from heat and put through strainer. Bring 3 cups of milk to boil and then add in ¼ pound butter, salt to taste, the grated cheese and, lastly, the rest of the milk in which the cornstarch has been dissolved. Stir constantly until mixture thickens. Remove from heat and divide into 2 parts. Add into the first part the grated carrots and heat, stirring constantly for 5 minutes. Then place this portion into a buttered baking dish. To the other portion, add the strained peas, mix well and then pour over the top of the first portion. Peel the potatoes and cook in little water. Then mash, forming a purée, with butter, egg yolks and a little milk. Place this mixture over the top and garnish with olives and tomato slices. Sprinkle with butter chips and dust with grated cheese. Bake in a hot oven until golden brown and serve hot.

VEGETABLE PUDDING

1 cup carrots, cooked and chopped
1 cup string beans, cooked and cut French style
1 cup potatoes, cooked and chopped
1 onion grated
2 cups milk
1 cup flour, salted to taste
4 eggs
1 tablespoon butter
3 tablespoons grated Parmesan cheese
1 tablespoon bread crumbs
1 apple, diced

COMBINE the milk, salt and flour and cook over low flame, stirring constantly until mixture thickens. Remove from heat and add the egg yolks mixing carefully so the mixture is smooth and free of lumps. Add the vegetables, butter, grated onion, cheese and lastly the beaten egg whites and the diced apples. Butter a pyrex baking dish and sprinkle with the bread crumbs. Pour in the mixture and bake in a medium oven until done. Turn out and serve, adding tomato sauce if desired.

VEGETABLE PRESERVES

4 *carrots*
5 *small cucumbers*
1 *cauliflower*
1 *cup olive oil*
1 *white turnip*
¼ *pound string beans*
4 *green peppers*
5 *scallions*
  vinegar, salt and pepper and any additional
  vegetables desired

PEEL and wash the vegetables. Then, boil in enough vinegar to cover. After boiling a few minutes, remove from heat and let cool, leaving in the pot and covered. The next day add the salt and peppers and boil again for a few minutes, removing from heat and cooling. Repeat this 4 times on four successive days. Drain thoroughly and place in a sterilized glass jar. Cover with fresh vinegar and 1 cup of olive oil. Keep for 10 days before using.

SAUCES and FILLINGS

"There is no sauce in the world like hunger."

Miguel Cervantes said this and, while we share the world's admiration for Spain's greatest writer, we think his culinary methods are questionable. On this basis, your dinner party is bound to be a huge success if you invite your guests to dine, setting the hour at 6 o'clock —and then serve dinner at 10 p.m. By that time, most guests will eat shoe leather with relish ... if they haven't already left for more nourishing pastures.

A better way to ensure the success of your meals is to enliven them with any of the recipes that follow for sauces and fillings. You won't have to rely on hunger, for these sauces are guaranteed to revive even the most jaded appetites.

SECTION ELEVEN

..............................SAUCES and FILLINGS..........................

BARBECUE SAUCE

vinegar
juice of 1 lemon
plenty of chopped onion
hot peppers

Mix ALL the ingredients together thoroughly and let stand a while before serving. If a milder sauce is desired, add a little water with salt to taste.

CHEESE SAUCE

¾ cups butter
3 cups milk
2 tablespoons flour
"ricotta" or pot cheese, as needed
3 egg yolks
black pepper to taste

COMBINE the milk, 2 tablespoons flour, the cheese and egg yolks in a bowl. Mix well and strain. Place mixture in pot and heat, adding butter and a little black pepper. Mix constantly to avoid sticking and cook well. When it is cooked and thickened, remove from heat. This sauce may be used with lasagna, macaroni or other "pasta" dishes as well as over toast, hardboiled eggs, boiled potatoes, vegetables, etc.

CHICKEN GRAVY

2 cups chicken broth
chicken giblets
condiments as desired
3 egg yolks
1 tablespoon butter
2 tablespoons flour
milk as needed

COOK the giblets in 8 cups water together with the chicken broth and condiments desired. When done, strain. There should be 4 cups of liquid obtained. If not, add milk. Into the gravy, mix the egg yolks, 1 tablespoon butter and the flour. Then heat until cooked and mixture thickens. When the chicken is ready, place on pyrex plate and cover with the gravy. Return to oven for a few minutes. Serve hot.

CHICKEN SAUCE

3 cups chicken broth
10 tablespoons grated Parmesan cheese
4 egg yolks
2 tablespoons butter
4 tablespoons flour
1½ cups milk
salt and black pepper to taste

162

STRAIN the chicken broth and pour into a pot with butter, egg yolks and flour which has been slowly dissolved in the milk. Add salt and black pepper to taste. Stir constantly until the mixture thickens and is cooked. Then, add the grated cheese, mix well and leave for 5 more minutes over the flame before removing.

CHICKEN SAUCE WITH CREAM CHEESE

3 cups milk
¾ pounds cream cheese
2 tablespoons butter
4 egg yolks
2 tablespoons cornstarch or flour
salt to taste

COMBINE the cheese, 2 cups of milk, 2 tablespoons butter and a little salt in a pot and heat, stirring constantly until it reaches the boiling point. Then add the remaining cup of milk into which the 4 egg yolks and the flour have been well blended. Continue stirring constantly until mixture thickens. Cover the chicken with this sauce. It is also delicious over chicken croquettes.

CHICKEN SAUCE WITH PEAS

chicken drippings
2 cups milk
3 egg yolks
4 tablespoons grated cheese
2 level tablespoons flour
canned peas

Combine ingredients and heat until mixture thickens, stirring constantly. Arrange the chicken on a platter and cover with the sauce. Sprinkle the grated cheese and warmed canned peas on top.

CREAM AND TOMATO SAUCE

½ pound butter
2 onions, sliced
1 pound tomatoes
 salt, garlic and hot peppers to taste
1½ quarts unsweetened whipped cream

Heat the butter and when golden brown, add the sliced onions, the tomatoes, blended and strained, and salt, garlic and hot peppers to taste. When the sauce is thick, add in the unsweetened whipped cream. Boil a little more, until thickened and pour over chicken, beef or vegetable dishes.

HOT "FEIJOADA" SAUCE

2 tomatoes, peeled and seedless
 hot peppers, salt and garlic to taste
2 lemons, juiced
½ cup vinegar
2 onions, chopped fine
 scallion and parsley sprig, minced
1 cup of liquid from the "feijoada," strained

Put the tomatoes, hot peppers, salt and garlic through a blender. Place the blended ingredients in a serving dish and add the juice of 2 lemons, the chopped onions, the minced scallion and parsley and the vinegar. Lastly, when ready to serve, add the strained "feijoada"* liquid and mix lightly with the sauce.

BASIC SALAD SAUCE

FOR every 2 tablespoons of oil, mix in 1 tablespoon of vinegar, ½ teaspoon of grated onion, a little chopped parsley and salt to taste.

SÃO PAULO STEW SAUCE

lard
onion
tomatoes, sliced
garlic pressed in salt
carrots
green peppers, cut in lengthwise strips
black pepper and hot peppers to taste

HEAT a little lard and when very hot add the onion, chopped, the sliced tomatoes and the garlic and salt. When brown, add finely chopped carrots and plenty of green pepper strips along with the black pepper and hot peppers, minced. Add a little water to this mixture and boil until the sauce thickens. When ready to serve the São Paulo stew, arrange the meats in the middle of a large platter, surrounded by the vegetables, and cover with this sauce. This sauce may also be used over other meat dishes.

---

* See recipe on page 90.

SHRIMP SAUCE

2 *pounds shrimp*
1 *pound tomatoes, peeled and seedless*
1 *onion*
  salt, garlic and hot peppers to taste
  parsley sprig and scallion
  butter to fry the shrimp
  lemon juice

CLEAN and wash shrimp in water and lemon juice. Place the onion, peppers, tomatoes and 1 cup water in blender. When thoroughly blended, add the shrimp. Turn the blender on and off 3 times in rapid succession so that the shrimp become more or less broken up. Heat a little butter and when brown, add the shrimp mixture with salt and pepper to taste. Simmer long enough to cook the shrimp and to let the mixture become thick. When ready, remove from heat, let cool and pour into pastry shell or serve with rice or "pasta" dishes.

COLD SHRIMP SAUCE

1 *cup dried shrimp*
1 *cup dendê oil (or substitute olive oil)*
1 *onion*
1 *tablespoon cayenne peppers*

PUT DRY ingredients through meat grinder. Heat the oil in frying pan then add in the puréed ingredients, stirring continuously to prevent drying out. Serve cold.

TOMATO PASTE

2 *pounds ripe tomatoes*
1 *large onion, grated*
½ *pound pickles, dill*
3 *eggs*
1 *tablespoon mustard*
   hot peppers and black pepper to taste
½ *pound grated Parmesan cheeese*
½ *pound butter*
¼ *pound green olives, pitted*

Scald then peel the tomatoes and remove seeds. Heat ¼ pound of butter then add in the grated onion and sauté. Add in the tomatoes which have been put in the blender with 1 cup water, salt and pepper and a pinch of sugar. Simmer until water evaporates, making the mixture concentrated. Remove from stove and add beaten eggs (yolks and whites beaten separately). Mix well in order to stir in the eggs. Return to flame, adding the cheese and mustard. Let mixture thicken a little, remove from flame and, while still hot, add in the rest of the butter, the pickles and olives, chopped fine.

"TUCUPÍ" SAUCE
(Manioc Sauce)

4 *pounds manioc root*
1 *quart water*

Peel, wash and grate the manioc, placing the mixture in a cloth sack. Squeeze thoroughly into a separate dish. Then add in the water

167

to the manioc mixture and again squeeze thoroughly and set aside the resultant yellow liquid. Let the liquids stand for 2 hours then pour off the liquid portion slowly and very carefully in order to avoid disturbing the powder-like substance deposited on the bottom of the dish. This fermented liquid is the "tucupí" to which whole cayenne peppers may be added.

WHITE SAUCE

4 tablespoons cornstarch or flour
4 cups milk
4 egg yolks
2 tablespoons butter
salt and black pepper to taste

COMBINE the milk, flour and the egg yolks and pass through a fine strainer. Season with salt, black pepper and butter. Heat over a low flame, stirring constantly to avoid lumping, until the mixture cooks and forms a creamy sauce. When ready, remove from heat and use immediately. You may add some grated cheese or the milk from 1 coconut (see recipe on page 173) or both, if desired.

WINE AND TOMATO SAUCE

2 tablespoons butter or olive oil
1 grated onion
2 cloves pressed garlic
1 pound tomatoes
salt, black pepper and hot peppers to taste
1 or 2 cups white wine

PLACE 2 tablespoons butter or olive oil in a frying pan. Heat and add 1 grated onion and 2 cloves of pressed garlic. Sauté and then add 1 pound tomatoes which have been passed through blender. Add salt, hot peppers and black pepper to taste. Then add 1 or 2 cups of white wine and simmer until mixture thickens a little and some of the liquid evaporates. Serve this sauce over beef or fowl.

CHEESE FILLING

> *⅔ pounds bland cheese*
> *4 egg yolks and 4 egg whites, beaten until stiff*
> *1 tablespoon butter*
> *½ cup milk*

MIX ALL ingredients throughly and use to fill "empada" or pie shells.

CHICKEN FILLING

> *½ chicken*
> *1 tablespoon lard*
> *1 small onion*
> *1 clove garlic pressed in salt*
> *   hot peppers and black pepper, to taste*
> *   and parsley sprig, chopped*
> *1 scallion*
> *3 tomatoes, peeled and without seeds*

HEAT the lard and when hot, add the onion and tomatoes chopped together with pressed garlic and salt. Sauté lightly and add the chicken in parts, the parsley, scallion and water, little by little.

169

Simmer until the chicken is well cooked. When the chicken is ready, remove from flame, strain the liquid and set aside. Remove the bones from the chicken, shred the meat and add to the liquid. Heat again, letting the liquid evaporate. Thicken the sauce with flour mixed in a little milk. Stir constantly to avoid lumping. Simmer until the sauce is thick and of a smooth consistency. Cool and then use as filling for the chicken "empada" or chicken pie.

SHRIMP FILLING

> 1 pound shrimp
> 3 tomatoes
> 1 onion
> 1 can hearts of palm*
> 1 can peas
> scallion and parsley sprig
> garlic, salt, black pepper and hot peppers to taste
> ¼ pound flour
> ½ cup milk
> 1 egg yolk
> 1 tablespoon butter

HEAT 1 tablespoon butter. Add, the onion, chopped fine and the tomatoes, peeled and without seeds, and sauté. Then add in the shrimp, the condiments (as desired), hearts of palm, sliced, and 4 cups water. Simmer a while; then add in the peas and the scallion and parsley, chopped fine. Boil and thicken with a little flour, dissolved in a little milk, and 1 egg yolk. Stir until a cream sauce forms. Cool and use to fill pie shell or served with rice, etc.

---

* See "Glossary for Cooks" on page 247.

BEVERAGES

Section Twelve

························BEVERAGES·························

COCONUT MILK

Remove the shell of the coconut and grate the meat or place it in a blender. Press the meat of the coconut to get out as much of the milk as possible. Strain the milk through a cloth napkin, wringing the napkin to squeeze out the milk. This first liquid from the grated meat will be very thick and rich. Next add a little water to the pressed coconut milk, mix well and let stand a minute or two. Then press the coconut meat and repeat the procedure to squeeze out the coconut milk as before. This second liquid will be thinner than the first. Mixed together, the first and second liquid will yield between ¾ and 1 cup of coconut milk.

MATTE TEA

Brew matte tea just like you brew ordinary tea. Three-quarters of an ounce of matte is sufficient for about one quart of beverage. For a good cup of hot matte tea, use one teaspoonful of the burnt type of matte or two teaspoonsful of the green type to a cup of hot water. Let brew for a few minutes until desired strength is attained. Then strain and add sugar if desired. Hot milk may also be used in place of the hot water.

ICED MATTE TEA

BREW the matte as for the hot drink and either cool by adding ice cubes or placing in the refrigerator. For foamy matte, mix in an electric beater or in a cocktail shaker and serve. A few drops of lemon juice will enhance the taste.

COPACABANA DRINK

> 1 small glass rum
> 1 glass iced matte
> lemon juice drops to taste

PUT THE rum and the lemon juice drops along with the iced matte in a blender or cocktail shaker and mix well. Whiskey or cognac may be substituted for the rum if desired.

PINEAPPLE RUM PUNCH

> 2 fresh pineapples
> 8 glasses of cold water
> sugar to taste
> 1 glass rum
> 1 glass white wine
> fresh strawberries as desired

REMOVE the pineapple skins, set aside ¼ of a pineapple and grate the remaining pineapple or cut into medium size pieces and put through a blender with the water. Strain the blended pineapple and add sugar to taste. Fill an ice cube tray with the pineapple juice and put in the freezer. Place the remaining pineapple juice in the refrigerator to cool until ready to serve. Slice the strawberries and cut the remaining ¼ pineapple into ½ inch pieces, sprinkle both with sugar and place in the refrigerator. When ready to serve, add the pineapple ice cubes, the strawberry and pineapple pieces, the white wine, and the rum to the pineapple juice and mix well. Serve with a sprig of mint if desired.

COCONUT RUM DRINK

1 large coconut
milk from one coconut
rum, cognac, brandy or cachaça (if available)

CUT THE top off the large coconut and remove the liquid from inside. Pour the coconut milk (see recipe on page 173) into the coconut and add as much of the brandy, rum, cognac or cachaça as the coconut will hold. Place in the refrigerator and let stand for one or two weeks —the longer the better— before serving.

QUENTÃO
(Hot Rum Punch)

rum or cachaça (if available)
cloves
cinnamon
lemon slices
sugar to taste
water

175

FÓR EVERY cupful of rum, add one clove, one cinnamon stick, one lemon slice and ½ cup of water. Place all ingredients in a pot and heat until just about to boil. Serve hot in mugs.

"CAIPIRINHA"*
(Brazilian "Moonshine")

rum or cachaça (if available)
lemon juice
lemon rind, grated
sugar to taste
crushed ice

FOR EVERY jigger of rum, add a jigger of lemon juice. Sprinkle the grated lemon rind with a little sugar and add to the lemon and rum mixture. Serve poured over a little crushed ice. If preferred, strain the rum and lemon juice mixture to remove the lemon rind before serving.

---

* "Caipirinha" is a drink which originated in the Brazilian "back hills" among the Brazilian "hillbillies"—but it didn't take long to become popular among the sophisticated "city slickers."

CAKES and PASTRIES

In Brazil, next to The Unpardonable Sin of not serving coffee after dinner, comes the sin of not serving dessert. For, Brazil is a land of sweet-toothed citizens and their desserts —like the innumerable cups of cafézinho they drink— are sweet, very sweet. This may be the reason why Brazil has grown to be the world's second largest producer of cane sugar —simply to keep its own citizens happy.

In any case, for some years previous to 1960, while Brazilian production of sugar grew, its national consumption increased at such a rate that, oddly enough, exports of sugar decreased. Today, with Cuban sugar being diverted to the communist block, Brazil probably ranks first as supplier of cane sugar to the Western countries. —And its citizens probably continue to consume more sugar per capita than any other country in South America.

Brazilians, in truth, do fantastic things with sugar such as, for example, convert humble hominy into a delicious dessert or make candy out of pumpkin squares and sweet potatoes. Their talents for making desserts and sweets is such that some of their cookbooks devote almost half their pages to the art. The recipes that are given here and in the following three sections have been carefully selected from among a host of others so that you can have an idea —and taste a sampling— of the wide range of Brazilian desserts.

SECTION THIRTEEN

···CAKES and PASTRIES···

BROWN ANGELFOOD CAKE

12 eggs, separated
12 tablespoons sugar
12 tablespoons bread crumbs

Beat egg whites until stiff. Add in the egg yolks, beat very well and then add in the sugar and continue beating. Lastly, add in the bread crumbs. Bake in a hot oven in a buttered angelfood cake pan. When done, slice into 3 layers and cover with the following sauce:

Chocolate Sauce

1½ cups milk
¼ pound sugar
2 tablespoons cocoa

Heat the milk and then add in the sugar and cocoa. When mixture comes to a boil remove from heat. When cooled a little, but still warm, add in the rum. Cover each layer with the chocolate sauce. Then combine the layers and cover entire cake with the walnut butter icing on the following page.

Walnut Butter Icing

½ pound butter
2 egg yolks
1 pound sugar
⅛ pound grated Parmesan cheese
½ pound ground walnuts

CREAM the butter, sugar and egg yolks. Add in the cheese and nuts. Mix very well and then frost the cake. Place in the refrigerator for a few hours and serve chilled.

BANANA CAKE

1 dozen bananas
powdered cinnamon to taste
1 pound sugar
2 cups flour
1 cup milk
1 cup butter
3 eggs, separated
1 tablespoon baking powder

PEEL and slice bananas lengthwise. Butter a baking form and sprinkle with cinnamon. Then arrange the bananas with a layer of sugar between each layer of banana. Fill the form about halfway, pressing the banana layers together so no space is left. There should be about a space of about 1½ inches from the top for the dough. To make the dough, cream the butter and 1 cup sugar. Add in the egg yolks and continue beating. Add in the milk and flour. Beat very well and lastly add in the egg whites, beaten, and the baking powder. Bake in a hot oven and, when ready, cut into squares.

"FLAVITA" BANANA CAKE

1 cup butter
2 cups sugar
3 eggs
3 cups flour
1 cup milk
1 tablespoon baking powder
grated lime peel

CREAM the butter and sugar, add in the egg yolks and continue beating. Little by little, add in the milk and flour and beat well. Add in the egg whites, beaten and lastly the baking powder and grated lemon peel. Next, prepare the banana filling below.

Banana Filling

12 heaping tablespoons sugar
½ cup sweet wine
6 to 8 bananas, sliced
¼ pound pitted prunes, chopped

HEAT the sugar until it turns golden brown and then add in the wine and prunes. When mixture boils, remove from heat. Grease a baking form with butter and pour in the prune mixture and slices of banana. Then pour the dough mixture on top. Place form in a tray of water and bake until done.

CHOCOLATE CAKE "IRENE"

1 cup butter
3 cups flour
2½ cups sugar
1 cup cocoa
4 eggs
1 heaping tablespoon baking powder
1 cup milk

CREAM the butter and sugar very well; then add in the egg yolks, beating constantly. Stir in the cocoa mixed in with the milk and flour. Lastly, add in the egg whites beaten until stiff. Sift in the baking powder. Mix batter lightly and bake in a buttered baking tray. When done, cut in half, lengthwise. Spread with the following:

Chocolate Filling

2 cups sugar
2 cups water
6 egg yolks, beaten
2 tablespoons butter
1 cup chocolate
½ teaspoon vanilla

PREPARE a stringy syrup by heating the sugar and water until the mixture thickens. Remove from heat and add in the butter, chocolate and the beaten egg yolks. Stir in rapidly and return to heat. When mixture thickens and boils, remove from heat and, while still hot, use for cake filling and icing.

182

COLD "MARIELA" CAKE

Chocolate Wine Sauce

6 cups water
3 cups sugar
8 tablespoons cocoa
2 cups port wine

COMBINE all ingredients except wine. Bring to a boil. When mixture begins to thicken, remove from flame and let cool. Add in 2 cups port wine.

Butter Cream Frosting

1 pound butter
5 cups sugar
6 egg yolks

CREAM the butter and sugar until consistent; then slowly add in the egg yolks and continue to beat until mixture whitens and loses the taste of the eggs.

Cake

3¼ pounds lady fingers
2 pounds shelled walnuts, ground

MOISTEN the lady fingers in the chocolate wine sauce, one at a time, without letting them break. Arrange 1 layer of the lady fingers in a plate in any form desired. Then pour on 1 layer of the butter cream, sprinkle liberally with nuts, then add another layer of the lady fingers dipped in the chocolate wine sauce and continue until all the lady fingers are used up. Cover completely with the butter cream, sprinkle with ground nuts and garnish with some chopped nuts. Cover the plate entirely with wax paper or aluminum foil and chill for 24 hours.

CORN MEAL CAKE

1 quart of milk
4 cups corn meal
2 cups sugar
1 cup butter
1 clove
  eggs as needed
  pinch of salt
  anise
  cinnamon stick
  nutmeg

BRING milk to a boil with the salt and spices, strain and set to boil again. Sift the corn meal and add to the milk. Stir constantly to avoid lumps. Add in the butter and sugar. Remove from heat and let cool slightly. When warm, add in the whole eggs beaten, enough to make a batter of a consistency for a cake mixture. Bake in a buttered baking dish in a hot oven.

CORN MEAL CAKE WITH CHEESE

1 cup milk
1 cup corn meal
1 cup sugar
1 cup grated cheese
2 heaping tablespoons butter
4 eggs, beaten separately
1 tablespoon baking powder

CREAM the butter and sugar, then add in the egg yolks and beat well. Add in the milk, the corn meal, the cheese and, lastly, the egg whites beaten until stiff and sift in the baking powder. Mix well and bake in a buttered cake pan in a hot oven.

MOCK ENGLISH FRUIT CAKE

½ pound sugar
½ pound flour
3 eggs, separated
½ pound mixed of walnuts and dried minced candied
   fruits (such as pineapple, raisins, figs, oranges,
   prunes, apricots, etc.)
1 cup port wine
¼ pound butter
1 level teaspoon baking powder

CREAM the butter with the sugar very well. Then beat in the egg yolks, flour and the minced candied fruits (dipped in a little flour so that they do not stick together) and the nuts. Next, beat the egg

185

whites until stiff and add in. Lastly, add the port wine and beat the ingredients well until the batter starts to bubble. Add in the baking powder, sifted and sprinkled on top of the dough. Mix well and bake in a hot oven in a buttered, tubular cake form.

THERESA'S FRUIT CAKE

2 apples
1 ripe peach, peeled and diced
¼ pound pitted prunes
¼ pound seedless raisins
1 banana, sliced thick
1 jigger sweet wine or rum
⅔ pound sugar

CUT APPLES in half, remove seeds and then cut each half in two so that there are 4 large slices. Place in water with lemon juice so they do not turn brown. Caramelize the sugar a little, then add in 4 cups water and let boil a little. Add in the prunes, raisins and peach. Boil a little more without letting mixture thicken very much. Remove from heat and add in the wine. Arrange in decorative fashion, the apple slices, bananas slices and prune mixture in a large baking dish. Cover with angelfood batter made as follows:

Angelfood Cake

5 eggs, separated
5 tablespoons sugar
4 tablespoons flour

BEAT egg whites until stiff. Add in the yolks and sugar and then beat well until mixture whitens. Next, fold in the flour. Pour this batter over fruit mixture and bake in a low oven. When done, let cool and then turn out and serve chilled.

HONEY LOAF "CARAMURÚ"

6 *cups flour*
3 *cups sugar*
2 *cups honey*
2 *cups milk*
3 *teaspoons cinnamon*
3 *tablespoons butter*
2 *teaspoons baking soda*
6 *cloves, ground*

CREAM the butter and sugar. Then continuing to beat, slowly add in the flour, honey, baking soda, cinnamon and cloves, ground and sifted. Lastly, add in the milk. Beat very well and bake in a hot oven in a loaf pan lined with wax paper. Remove when done and when almost cold, cover with the following icing:

Chocolate Icing

1¼ *cups sugar*
2 *tablespoons milk*
2 *tablespoons butter*
½ *cup cocoa*
    pinch of salt
    a few drops of vanilla extract

COMBINE ingredients and mix well. Heat over low flame, stirring continuously for about 6 minutes or until mixture thickens. Remove from heat, beat until mixture cools a little and then pour over the honey loaf. Cut in slices.

PRUNE CAKE

1 cup butter
2 cups sugar
4 eggs
1⅓ cups milk
3 cups flour
1⅓ cups prune whip
2 tablespoons baking powder
nutmeg to taste
2 cloves, ground
pinch of salt
powdered cinnamon to taste
1 tablespoon bread crumbs
lemon peel, grated

CREAM the butter and sugar and then add in the egg yolks, prune whip (see recipe below), milk, flour sifted with the baking powder, cinnamon, nutmeg and ground cloves. Lastly, add in the egg whites beaten until stiff and grated peel of ½ lemon and bread crumbs. Bake in buttered baking dish in hot oven.

Prune Whip

½ pound pitted prunes
1 cup sugar
1 cup water

HEAT the pitted prunes, sugar and water and let simmer until liquid almost evaporates. Then beat in a blender.

SLICES OF HEAVEN

4 whole eggs and 1 yolk
½ cup orange juice or water
2 cups sugar
2 cups flour
1 teaspoon baking powder

BEAT the egg yolks well. Add in the orange juice or water followed by the sugar and beat until the mixture is of a creamy consistency. Add in the flour, sifted with the baking powder. Lastly, add in the egg whites beaten until fluffy. Bake in a hot oven in a form lined with wax paper. When done, cut in diamond shapes and prepare the following sauce:

Wine Sauce

1¼ pounds sugar
1 tablespoon honey
3 cups water
1 cups wine or rum

HEAT all ingredients. When mixture begins to boil, dip in the cakes a few at a time and let cook a little while. Then remove with a pierced spoon. Serve very cold.

PETRÓPOLIS BREAD

2 cakes of brewer's yeast
1 quart milk
1 pound flour
1 level tablespoon salt
2 tablespoons anise
  cinnamon stick
10 eggs
⅔ pound butter
½ pound pork lard
¾ cups sugar
  flour sufficient for kneading

DISSOLVE the brewer's yeast and 1 tablespoon sugar in 3 cups milk; then add in 1 pound flour, beat very well and let stand for 1½ hours. Then beat the eggs and sugar together and add to the dough after it has risen. Also add in the butter and lard. Separately, bring to a boil the 1 cup of milk remaining and add in the 2 tablespoons of anise, the cinnamon stick, salt and a little nutmeg. When the mixture boils, remove from heat and let cool. Strain and then add to the dough mixture. Knead very well and sprinkle in a little flour until mixture no longer stricks to your hands and can be rolled out. Let stand about 20 minutes. Knead again and then divide the dough into sizes and shapes desired — in ring or braided. When ready to roll out, chopped nuts and seedless raisins may be added. Roll out and place in buttered baking sheet. Cover with a napkin and let stand until the rolls have risen some more and they are nice and light. Place a little ball of dough in a glass of water in the same place where the bread has been placed to raise. When the ball of dough, rises to the top of the water, the bread is ready for baking. Bake in a hot oven. When almost done, remove for a few minutes and brush with egg yolks mixed in a little butter and sprinkle with crystalized sugar. Return to the oven to finish baking.

ECONOMY COOKIES

4 cups arrowroot
2 whole eggs
2 tablespoons butter
  pinch of salt
2 cups sugar

COMBINE ingredients and knead well until mixture sticks together and is soft. Roll out into small lengths and slice or cut out with cookie forms. Press the fork tines on top of each cookie for decoration. Bake on a buttered cookie sheet until golden brown.

COUNTRY STYLE JELLY COOKIES

¾ pound flour
⅓ pound sugar
⅓ pound butter
4 egg yolks
1 tablespoon baking powder
  melted jelly or guava paste as needed

CREAM the butter and sugar, add in the egg yolks, and baking powder sifted together with the flour. Mix well and knead. Then form into little balls about the size of walnuts. Press down in the

191

center with a cork or your thumb to make a cavity and bake. When done, fill the cavity with jelly. The cookies may be kept and filled only when served.

BAHIA CUPCAKES

½ pound butter
½ pound sugar
6 eggs, separated
½ pound rice flour
½ grated coconut

CREAM the butter and sugar, add in the egg yolks and then the egg whites, beaten. Add in the rice flour and grated coconut and mix well. Bake in paper cupcake shells.

MOTHER BENTA CUPCAKES, PERNAMBUCO STYLE

¾ pound butter
¾ pound sugar
¾ pound rice flour
1 large coconut, grated
½ teaspoon salt
raisins
8 eggs (4 yolks and 4 whole)

GRATE the coconut and divided into two equal portions. From one of the portions strain out all of the coconut milk (see recipe on page 173). Then, cream the butter and sugar, add in the egg yolks and continue beating. Add in the coconut milk, the grated coconut, the egg whites beaten until stiff and, lastly, the rice flour. Add in ½ teaspoon of salt. Mix well and drop into patty shells. Place a raisin in each form, place the shells in aluminum forms and place the forms on a tray. Bake in hot oven. Serve each in a paper patty shell.

MOTHER BENTA'S THRIFTY CUPCAKES

⅓ *pound butter*
½ *pound sugar*
1 *pound rice flour*
4 *eggs, separated*
2 *tablespoons milk*

CREAM butter and sugar, add in the egg yolks, milk and continue beating. Fold in the rice flour and then the egg whites, beaten. Bake in a hot oven in paper cupcake shells.

PEANUT LOAF

6 *eggs*
¾ *cups sugar*
½ *pound roasted peanuts, ground*
6 *tablespoons bread crumbs*

BEAT egg whites until stiff and then sift in the sugar and beat again until stiff. Add in the bread crumbs, mix thoroughly and add in the peanuts. Mix well and bake in hot oven in a buttered baking sheet, wrapped in foil. When done, remove the foil and slice the loaf in half. Spread with the coffee filling on the following page.

193

Coffee Filling

¼ *pound butter*
2 *egg yolks*
1 *cup roasted ground peanuts*
3 *tablespoons strong coffe*
10 *heaping tablespoons sugar*

BEAT the butter and the egg yolks very well then add in the coffee and sugar. Beat very well and add in the peanuts. Mix well and use for filling and topping. Garnish loaf with peanut halves and place in refrigerator for about ½ hour so that the filling becomes firm before serving.

APPLE, CHEESE AND NUT PIE

¼ *pound butter*
1 *whole egg*
1 *egg yolk*
¼ *pound sugar*
3 *tablespoons milk*
1 *level tablespoon baking powder*
flour as needed

CREAM butter and sugar then add in the eggs beaten, the milk, baking powder and flour sufficient to make a dough of soft consistency but firm enough not to stick to fingers. Divide the dough in half and roll out so that one portion will be larger than the other. Using the larger portion, line a pie pan, greased, and fill with the apple and nut filling on the following page.

Apple and Nut Filling

3 green apples
½ cup walnuts
sugar and rum to taste

CHOP 3 green apples into small pieces and cook with a little sugar, a little rum and ½ cup walnuts, chopped. When almost dry and water almost evaporated remove from flame and let cool then pour into lined pie pan. Using the smaller portion of dough, cover and bake in medium oven until done. Then sprinkle on top ½ cup grated American or other bland cheese and return to oven until cheese melts. Serve hot.

BANANA SQUARES

12 bananas
1¾ cups sugar
2 tablespoons butter
2 tablespoons powdered chocolate

USING a fork, mash the bananas well and mix with the sugar, butter, chocolate. Heat in a pan and continue mixing until mixture sticks together. Beat then pour onto a buttered baking sheet and cut into squares.

CORN MEAL SQUARES

8 *eggs, separated*
8 *tablespoons butter*
8 *tablespoons sugar*
1 *heaping tablespoon baking powder*
2 *tablespoons grated Parmesan cheese*
12 *tablespoons corn meal*
½ *teaspoon grated lemon peel*
pinch of salt

SIFT the corn meal, sugar, salt and baking powder. Beat the butter with the egg yolks then add in the dry ingredients and lastly, add in the egg whites, beaten, and the cheese. Mix well and bake in a pan on a buttered baking sheet, in hot oven. When done, cut into diamond shapes or whatever other shape desired. If desired, the following orange icing may be spread on top before cutting.

Orange Icing

To 1 cup orange juice add in enough sugar to make mixture very thick. Beat very well and then spread on top of the cake.

CORN INDIAN STYLE

24 *ears of corn*
1 *tablespoon butter, salted*
1 *quart milk or 1 quart water*
plenty of sugar

GRATE the ears of corn and add the milk or water. Then dip the ears in a little milk and scrape with a knife well so as to extract all the corn. Put the corn mixture through a coarse strainer, add in plenty of sugar and the butter, melted, and mix very well. Remove some of the green leaves from the corn husks and sew together to form sacks. Spoon the corn mixture into these sacks and tie the open ends with pieces of corn silk or light string. Drop the sacks into boiling water and let cook. When the leaves turn yellow, it is a sign that the corn is cooked. Remove from heat, drain off the water and let cool. Serve in the husks.

BAHIAN DELIGHTS

> 1 *pound sugar*
> 20 *egg yolks*
> 1 *grated coconut*
> 2 *tablespoons butter*
> 1 *level tablespoon flour*

MAKE a stringy syrup by heating the sugar in 2 cups water. Add in the butter and, when cold, add in the grated coconut and the egg yolks and flour, sifted. Mix very well and bake in a hot oven in buttered forms placed in a tray of hot water. When ready, let cool and then turn out and place in paper patty shells.

GRANDMA'S PETITE FOURS

1½ *pounds sugar*
1½ *pounds arrowroot*
9 *whole eggs, separated*
9 *egg yolks*

COMBINE the sugar and egg yolks. Beat well and sift in the arrowroot, beating continuously. Then add in the egg whites, beaten. Beat until mixture begins to emit air bubbles. Bake in a hot oven in buttered baking tins.

CANDIES

CANDIES

ANGEL'S KISSES

1 dozen egg yolks
2 pounds sugar
4 cups water

Bᴇᴀᴛ the egg yolks until thick (almost stiff) and pour into buttered muffin tins. Bake a few minutes until the "kisses" become dry. Meanwhile make a syrup by boiling the sugar in the water until the mixture thickens. The syrup should be boiling when the "kisses" are removed from the oven. Using a toothpick, lift the "kisses" from the baking form and dip in the syrup until they become throughly impregnated with the syrup. Serve in fancy pastry shells.

ANITA'S DREAMS

3 cups flour
1 pint water
1 tablespoon butter
6 eggs
½ teaspoon salt
1 pound sugar
1 cup water
1 wine glass of rum or port wine

HEAT the water, salt and butter. When boiling, add in the flour and stir rapidly so as to avoid lumping. Continue stirring constantly until the mixture becomes quite thick and lifts easily from the bottom of the pot. Remove from heat and let cool a while. Then add in the eggs, one at a time, beating the mixture after each egg is added until the mixture becomes soft. (The mixture, however, should not become too soft.) Then heat plenty of lard in a large pan (as for southern frying), and when the lard becomes very hot, drop in the "dreams," using two tablespoons to pick up the batter. Cover the pan and remove from direct heat until the "dreams" puff up. Then, return to the heat, uncovered, so that they brown. When the "dreams" are brown, remove from pan and place on a paper towel to drain off the excess lard. Meanwhile, prepare a syrup by boiling together the sugar and the cup of water. When the syrup begins to thicken, remove from the heat, add in the rum or wine and let cool a while. Then, place the "dreams in a deep dish and cover with the syrup. Keep in the refrigerator until the following day when the "dreams" should be served cold.

BROWN EYED SUSANS

2 pounds almonds, shelled and ground
1 pound sugar
10 egg yolks
3 tablespoons cocoa
½ teaspoon vanilla

PREPARE a thick syrup by heating the sugar in water, add in the almonds and leave over flame to thicken a little more. Remove from heat, let cool and add in the egg yolks, beaten with the vanilla. Mix very well and divide mixture into 2 parts, placing each in a pot. To one part sift in the cocoa and heat, mixing continuously until mixture sticks together. Do not overcook so that the mixture doesn't crystallize. Let stand to cool a little. Proceed in the same way with the other portion, except that the cocoa is not included. When ready, remove from flame and let cool a little. Form into little balls, the brown ones smaller than the yellow ones. Then press one brown ball on top of a yellow one and dip in crystalized sugar. Serve in paper patty shells.

REALLY DIFFERENT COCONUT BITES

> 6 eggs
> 6 tablespoons sugar
> 5 level tablespoons flour
> 6 tablespoons grated coconut
> 6 level tablespoons butter

BEAT the eggs well. Add in the sugar, flour, coconut and butter. Mix well and pour into muffin tins or some other appropriate baking form, buttered and floured. Bake in a medium oven. Turn out when cold and place in paper patty shells.

COCONUT BALLS OF SUNSHINE

> 1 grated coconut
>   sugar equal to the amount of grated coconut
> 2 egg whites, unbeaten

MEASURE out the grated coconut and combine with the same amount of sugar. Add in the egg whites and mix very well. Form into little balls and place in sun to dry on a cookie sheet sprinkled with crystallized sugar.

COFFEE ROLLS

1½ cups milk
1 cup strong coffee
3 cups sugar
1 heaping tablespoon butter
6 tablespoons honey
1 level tablespoon flour
1 egg yolk

COMBINE ingredients and heat until hard candy mixture forms. Pour onto a buttered cookie sheet, roll into long rolls and cut. Wrap in foil paper.

EGG STRINGS OR BIRD NESTS

24 egg yolks
4¼ pounds crystalized sugar
2 tablespoons orange essence, if desired

COMBINE the sugar and 5½ cups water and make a thin syrup. Put the egg yolks through a fine strainer 4 times and then add in the essence of orange. When the syrup is boiling, make the egg strings, preferably by pouring the egg mixture through a funnel with a thin hole. As the strings are cooked, remove from the syrup with a pierced tablespoon and strain off excess liquid by placing strings in a fine strainer moistened with cold water. Then spread out the strings carefully. Continue until all the mixture has been cooked,

then arrange as desired for serving, for example, as small birds'
nests or use to tie around snacks or for other decorative purposes
for a party table.

˙GOLDEN DREAMS

2 *large cans sweetened condensed milk*
⅔ *pound grated coconut, dried*
6 *egg yolks*
1 *tablespoon grated Parmesan cheese*
½ *pound chopped walnuts*

PLACE the cans of condensed milk, closed, in a pot with plenty of
water and boil for 2½ hours or for ½ hour in pressure cooker with
a pint of water. Let cool very well. Remove the condensed milk from
the cans and place in a pot. Add in the coconut, the egg yolks, the
cheese and a little vanilla extract. Mix very well and heat until mixture sticks together. Pour into buttered baking sheet and let cool.
When cold, form into little balls which are filled with the chopped
nuts. Then, roll in chocolate sprinkles or in crystalized sugar.

HONEY ROLLS

4 *cups milk*
3 *cups sugar*
½ *cup honey*
1 *tablespoon butter*
1 *tablespoon flour*
1 *egg yolk*
½ *teaspoon baking soda*

MIX THE flour with the milk and egg yolk and pass through a strainer. Put in a pot and add in the sugar and baking soda. Then heat, stirring constantly. When mixture is boiling and has thickened, add in the honey. Continue to mix until hard candy mixture is formed. Pour onto buttered cookie sheet, roll into long rolls and cut while hot. Place in foil forms.

MERINGUE SURPRISES

     5 egg whites
     1 pound sugar
     1 pound arrowroot
       few drops vanilla extract
     1 level tablespoon of baker's ammonia
       (or ammonium carbonate)

BEAT egg whites until stiff, add in the sugar and beat well. Then add in the arrowroot, vanilla and Baker's ammonia. Knead well and let stand for 2 hours. Form into little balls and place in a cookie sheet well apart since the "surprises" will expand.

MORE MERINGUE SURPRISES

     1 pound arrowroot
     ¾ pound sugar
     1 tablespoon baker's ammonia
     ½ teaspoon salt
     ½ teaspoon vanilla
     6 eggs whites

PREPARE exactly as above.

BAHIA MERINGUE

8 *egg whites*
1 *pound sugar*
½ *pound grated coconut*
3 *tablespoons ground peanuts*
½ *lemon peel*

BEAT egg whites until stiff and then add in the sugar and beat again until firm. Add in the grated coconut and ground peanuts, mix very well and spoon mixture into paper patty shells and place these in tin forms. Bake in a low oven.

DATE AND WALNUT DELIGHT

½ *pound walnuts, ground*
½ *pound dates, chopped fine*
½ *pound sugar*
6 *eggs*
1 *tablespoon baking powder*

BEAT the egg whites until stiff. Then add in the egg yolks and then the sugar. Beat well before adding in the ground walnuts (setting some aside for later) and dates. Mix well and then fold in the baking powder, mixing lightly. Place in a buttered baking tray and bake in a hot oven. When done and while still hot, cover with a chocolate glacé (see recipe on the following page) and sprinkle with the ground nuts. Chill, then cut into squares and serve in paper patty shells.

Chocolate Glacé

7 tablespoons sugar
1 cup water
2 tablespoons chocolate
1 tablespoons butter

Prepare a stringy syrup by heating the sugar and water together until the mixture starts to thicken. Remove from heat and then add in the chocolate and butter, beating slightly. Spread the chocolate glacé over the "Date and Walnut Delights."

A glacé may also be made by adding lemon juice to the thickened water and sugar syrup. Beat this glacé well before pouring over the "delights."

BOXED WALNUTS

½ pound ground walnuts
½ pound sugar
4 egg whites, beaten
a few drops lemon

Beat egg whites until fluffy, then sift in the sugar and beat until stiff. Add in the ground walnuts and drops of lemon. Mix well and, using 2 small spoons, drop into paper patty shells. Dry in low oven for a few minutes and serve in the shells.

PECAN CANDY ROLLS

1 quart milk
3 cups sugar
1 cup honey
½ pound pecans, ground
½ teaspoon baking soda
1 tablespoon butter

COMBINE ingredients, mix well and heat, stirring constantly. When mixture starts to thicken, add the ground pecans and continue to stir until mixture starts to form a ball. Then, remove from flame, pour onto buttered cookie sheet, roll into long rolls and cut to the size desired.

NINITA'S MOCK CASHEW FRUIT

2 pounds sugar
12 whole eggs
1 grated coconut
1 pound peanuts, ground

PREPARE a stringy syrup by boiling the sugar in water. When ready, add in the coconut and the peanuts and remove from heat. Rapidly stir in the eggs, beaten and strained twice. Mix very well and return to heat until mixture sticks together. Remove from heat and let cool. When cold, shape the mixture into the form of the cashew fruit, dip in crystallized sugar and place a small whole almond in each "fruit," imitating a cashew nut.

PEANUT BRITTLE

2 pounds sugar
1 pound roasted, unsalted peanuts

HEAT the sugar over a very low flame and stir constantly until it melts into a thick syrup. Mix the peanuts in the syrup and when the mixture starts to become sugary, but before it hardens, beat the peanut brittle very well. Then, pour onto a buttered cookie sheet. When the brittle starts to harden, cut into squares. Then, let harden completely before eating.

WHITE PEANUT CANDY

1 cup Karo, white
3 cups sugar
1 cup water
3 egg whites
2 cups roasted peanuts, chopped

PREPARE a syrup by heating the sugar and water until a crust is formed. Separately beat the egg whites until stiff. Slowly, little by little, pour the hot syrup over the egg whites, beating continually until a firm mixture is formed. Then add in the peanuts. Mix well and pour into a buttered baking tray. Butter the fingers and, by hand, spread out the mixture over the tray and cut into squares immediately. When candy is hard, can and cover tightly so that it does not become soft and sugary. This is a delicious candy but it is difficult to prepare since it is hard to beat and success depends on how well it is beaten.

CANDIED PINEAPPLE CHIPS

1 sweet pineapple
2 pounds crystalized sugar
4 cups water

SLICE pineapple in ½ inch slices and wash well. Dip in boiling water, drain off and place in a china bowl. Prepare a thick syrup by boiling the sugar in 4 cups water. Pour the boiling mixture over the pineapple, cover the bowl tightly and let stand overnight. The following day, after 24 hours, remove the pineapple, and return liquid to flame. When boiling, pour again over the pineapple again cover tightly and let stand until the following day. Repeat this procedure for 7 days. On the 8th day, drain off the pineapple in a strainer, remove the hard center core of the pineapple and slice the pieces in triangular sections. Dip in crystallized sugar or granulated sugar and set out to dry.

PINEAPPLE AND RIPE PAPAYA BALLS

1 pineapple
1 ripe papaya
sugar

PEEL pineapple and put through a blender or meat grinder. Peel the papaya, remove seeds and mash very well with a fork. Measure out equal quantities of pineapple, papaya and sugar into a pot. Mix very well and heat, stirring constantly until mixture forms a soft ball. Remove from heat and let cool. Roll into small balls, dip in crystallized sugar and insert 1 clove in the middle of each. Serve in paper patty shells.

SWEET POTATO AND PINEAPPLE BALLS

2 pounds cooked sweet potatoes,
* pressed through a strainer*
1 small pineapple, peeled and put through meat grinder
* or in blender*
2 pounds sugar

COMBINE all ingredients, place in pot and heat, stirring constantly until mixture sticks together and becomes a shiny paste. Let cool then form into small balls and dip in crystallized sugar. Place in paper patty shells and place 1 clove in the center of each.

WHITE PINEAPPLE CANDY

1 fresh pineapple
sugar as needed

PEEL THE pineapple and liquefy in a blender or put through a meat grinder. Measure out the pineapple liquid and pulp together and combine with the same amount of sugar. Mix very well and heat, stirring continuously. Cook until a not too hard candy mixture is formed. Pour onto a buttered cookie sheet, spread out and cut. Wrap pieces in wax paper.

CUSTARDS
and PUDDINGS

SECTION FIFTEEN

.... CUSTARDS and PUDDINGS ....

COCONUT CUSTARD

1 grated coconut
12 egg yolks
¾ pounds sugar
2 tablespoons butter

P REPARE a paste with the sugar and 2 cups water. When ready, remove from heat and add in the butter. When the mixture is cold, add in the egg yolks, mix well and add in the grated coconut. Pour into buttered muffin tins, place in a tray of hot water and bake in a hot oven.

CRÈME DE CAFÉ

2 large cans sweetened condensed milk
1 cup milk
1 cup strong coffee
6 eggs

COMBINE the condensed milk, the milk, coffee and eggs, beaten. Then put the ingredients through a fine strainer 2 times. Pour into a form lined with caramelized sugar and place in a hot oven in a pan of hot water. Bake and serve.

HEAVENLY CRÈME

1 quart of milk
1 cup of cream
4 tablespoons cornstarch
1 jar strawberry jelly
4 egg yolks
 sugar as desired
⅔ pound lady fingers or similar cookies
2 cups sweet wine
½ teaspoon vanilla extract

COMBINE the milk, egg yolks and cornstarch in a bowl. Put through a fine strainer and then heat. Add in enough sugar to sweeten. Mix well and continue to stir while cooking to avoid lumps. When mixture beings to thicken, add in the cream and ½ teaspoon vanilla. Mix well, and when mixture begins to boil a little, remove from heat and arrange as follows using a deep pyrex dish: place 1 layer of lady fingers, moisten well with the wine, cover with plenty of the strawberry jelly and then cover with half of the prepared crème. On top place another layer of the lady fingers or other cookies, moistened with wine and cover with the strawberry jelly and finally the rest of the crème. Bake in a hot oven for 20 minutes. Then place in the refrigerator and serve chilled and sliced. This dish may be topped with prune syrup, (see recipe on page 223) or caramelized sugar.

COCONUT CRÈME

1 pound sugar
2 cups water
8 egg yolks
milk of 2 coconuts

PREPARE a thick syrup with the sugar and water. Remove from heat and let cool before adding in the egg yolks mixed in the coconut milk. Return to heat, stirring slowly until mixture thickens. This delicious crême has many uses, not only as a filling but also as a sauce for cakes and puddings.

CREAMED CORN

12 ears of corn
1 quart milk
1 heaping tablespoon butter
sugar and cinnamon to taste
1 grated coconut

CLEAN and grate the corn. Add in the milk and pass the mixture through a fine strainer. Flavor with plenty of sugar, add in the butter and heat, stirring constantly until the mixture thickens. When thickened add in the thick coconut milk extracted from the grated coconut and mix well until mixture forms a thick cream and is cooked. Pour into pyrex dish and sprinkle with plenty of powdered cinnamon. Serve cold.

217

COCONUT HOMINY, PERNAMBUCO STYLE

2 pounds hominy
milk of 3 coconuts
(keep thick and thin milks separated)*
1 pint milk
sugar and cinnamon to taste

SOAK the hominy overnight. On the following day, drain off the water and boil in plenty of fresh water. When cooked, and the water has almost all evaporated, add in the thin coconut milk mixed with the pint of plain milk. Then, add a little sugar and continue to cook a while longer. When cooked, and just before removing from heat, add in the thick coconut milk, stir, and when mixture begins to boil, remove from flame and serve. Do not let the mixture boil too much so that the milk does not evaporate and the mixture becomes thick. Serve hot.

FRIED BANANA PUDDING

12 medium size bananas for frying
4 eggs
2 cups sugar
1 cup grated Parmesan cheese
⅓ pound pitted black prunes
½ tablespoon butter
1 teaspoon vanilla
pinch of salt

---

* See recipe on page 173.

PEEL and slice the bananas lengthwise and fry in butter, olive oil or lard. Then place in a bowl. Beat the eggs and then add in together with the rest of the ingredients. Do not whip bananas but mix with other ingredientes. Caramelize sugar in a baking form and pour pudding batter into it. Then bake in a hot oven, placed in a tray of water.

COCONUT PUDDING

2 *pounds sugar*
10 *eggs*
5 *tablespoons flour*
1 *coconut, grated*
3 *tablespoons grated bland cheese*
2 *tablespoons butter*

PREPARE a thick syrup with the sugar and 4 cups water. Remove from heat, add in the butter and then let cool. Add in the eggs, beaten well, the grated coconut, the grated bland cheese and the flour. Mix well and then beat very well. Bake in a baking form lined with caramelized sugar and placed in a pan of hot water.

EGG WHITE PUDDING

6 *egg whites*
10 *tablespoons sugar*
juice and grated peel of 1 small lemon
¼ *pound black prunes*

BEAT the egg whites until fluffy. Add in the sugar, lemon juice and grated lemon peel and beat very well until stiff. Add in the prunes, cut in very small pieces. Bake in moderate oven in a form lined with caramelized sugar and placed in a tray of water.

GREEN PAPAYA PUDDING

2 medium size green papayas
3 pounds sugar

CUT the papaya in pieces and remove the seeds. Wash well and grate the entire fruit, both skin and pulp. After grating, wash well 3 times so that the papaya milk is removed. Place the grated papaya in a pot with plenty of water and cook until it becomes a little tender. Remove from heat, drain off all the water, squeeze thoroughly and rinse continually in running water so as to wash out the bitter, acid taste of the papaya milk. Prepare a thick syrup with the sugar and add in the grated papaya. Mix well and cook, stirring occasionally so that the mixture doesn't stick to the bottom of the pan, until the mixture thickens. Remove from heat and pour into custard dishes.

PUMPKIN PUDDING

1 pound pumpkin
3 tablespoons flour
1 wine glass of port wine
⅔ pound sugar
2 tablespoons butter
   thick milk of 1 coconut*
5 egg yolks
3 egg whites, beaten

QUARTER the pumpkin and cook in a little salted water. When tender, peel and put through a fine strainer. To this mixture add in the sugar, flour, butter, wine, eggs and coconut milk. Mix very well and press the mixture through a fine strainer 4 times. Bake in a form lined with caramelized sugar, placed in a tray with water.

BRAZILIAN RICE PUDDING

2 cups rice
6 egg yolks
1 quart milk
   sugar as desired

WASH the rice well and boil. As soon as it has almost cooked and has softened, add in the milk and sugar, stirring continuously so that it does not stick. When the rice has thoroughly cooked and the grains are separated, remove from heat, let cool a little and then

---

* See recipe on page 173.

add in the egg yolks, stirred in a little milk and passed through a fine strainer. Stir the strained egg yolk in rapidly so that the mixture doesn't curdle. Return to heat, stirring constantly until mixture forms a creamy texture. Remove from heat, pour in a serving dish and sprinkle with powdered cinnamon.

RICE PUDDING

½ pound rice
3 cups milk
4 egg yolks
1 teaspoon butter
sugar as desired

Cook the rice in water until done. Remove from flame and add in the egg yolks mixed in milk. Mix in well so that the egg yolks do not harden. Add in the sugar and heat until mixture sticks together. Pour into buttered baking dish and bake in a medium oven.

MISCELLANEOUS DESSERTS

SECTION SIXTEEN

·············· MISCELLANEOUS DESSERTS ··············

PRUNE SYRUP

½ pound sugar
2 cups water
prunes
wine or rum

CARAMELIZE the sugar a little and then add in the water. Let boil and add in prunes and a little wine or rum. When mixture thickens a little, remove from heat and cool.

GREEN PEACH COMPOTE

4¼ pounds large green gage peaches
3¼ pounds sugar

PEEL THE peaches and let boil in water for a few minutes. Drain off, let cool and place in clean water. Let stand for 2 hours. Meanwhile, make a thin syrup by boiling the sugar in water. Then add in the peaches which have been drained. Simmer over a low flame until the fruit is tender and completely impregnated with the syrup.

ORANGE COMPOTE

12 acid oranges
3¼ pounds sugar
cloves to taste

SCRAPE off the green peel of the oranges and partly quarter them so that you can remove the core and yet the oranges remain whole. Wash thoroughly and boil the scraped oranges for a few minutes. Drain off the water and let cool. Then place the oranges in fresh water. Keep changing the water for 3 or 4 days until all the bitter, acid taste has been removed. Then wash thoroughly. Make a thin syrup with the sugar then add in the orange and boil for a while. Remove from heat. The next day, boil again and let the syrup thicken. Then add in some cloves for flavor. When the syrup has become heavy and the oranges have become transparent, the orange compote is ready.

MANGO ICE CREAM

10 small ripe mangoes
3 egg whites
10 tablespoons sugar

BEAT egg whites until stiff, add in half the sugar and beat again until stiff. Then add in the rest of the sugar and continue beating until very stiff. Peel the mangoes and press through a strainer. To the liquid thus obtained add the same amount of water. Mix well and then add in the beaten egg whites being sure to mix these in well. Place in ice trays and put in freezer. When mixture begins to harden, remove, beat well and return to the freezer until ready to serve.

SÃO PAULO ICE CREAM

4 eggs, separated
1¼ cups sugar
1 quart warm milk
1 cup very strong (demitasse) coffee
½ pound roasted nuts, ground

BEAT the egg yolks and 1 cup of sugar in an electric mixer. Add in the milk and coffee. Remove from the mixer and then add in the egg whites which have been beaten stiff together with 4 tablespoons (¼ cup) of sugar. Mix well and fold in the roasted nuts. Place in the ice trays of the freezing compartment of your refrigerator, turn the thermostat setting up to freezing and let the ice cream freeze for 50 minutes. Then, remove the ice cream from the freezing compartment and beat well again in the mixer (at a slow speed) until the ice cream is soft and smooth and free of crystals. Place the ice cream in the freezing compartment again until ready to serve.

COCONUT GELATIN

5 *packages unflavored gelatin*
1 *package strawberry gelatin*
1 *can sweetened condensed milk*
    juice of ½ lemon
1 *pint coconut milk*
4 *egg whites*
4 *level tablespoons sugar*
2 *apples, peeled and diced*

BEAT egg whites until fluffy, add in the sugar and beat until very stiff. Dissolve the gelatin in a little boiling water and when cool, add in the egg whites. Mix well and then add in the condensed milk and coconut milk and mix well again. Next add in the lemon juice and diced apples. Pour into custard cups and place in the refrigerator to jell.

FROTHY CRÈME GELATIN

4 *packages unflavored gelatin*
1 *package strawberry gelatin*
5 *eggs, separated*
1½ *cups orange juice*
⅓ *pound sugar*

DISSOLVE the gelatin in hot water. Beat the egg yolks with sugar until light yellow. Then add in the orange juice, mix a little, and add in the dissolved gelatin. Lastly, add in the egg whites beaten until stiff and mix all ingredients well. Pour into mold greased with oil of sweet almonds and place in freezer. Turn out when ready to serve.

MARIA'S GELATIN

5 *egg whites*
2 *packages unflavored gelatin*
½ *package strawberry gelatin*
  a few drops of vanilla extract
1 *small coconut, grated fine*
6 *tablespoons sugar*

BEAT egg whites until fluffy. Add in sugar and beat until stiff. Add in the gelatin dissolved in a little hot water. Mix well and pour into forms lined with the grated coconut. Pour in evenly and cover with coconut. Place in refrigerator. When cold, cut into pieces and serve in paper shells.

STRAWBERRY GELATIN

2 *pounds fresh strawberries*
1 *cup orange juice*
5 *packages unflavored gelatin*
3 *packages strawberry gelatin*
1 *pound sugar*
1 *pound strawberries for garnish*
1 *pint cream or crème de chantilly*

229

DISSOLVE the gelatin in hot water. Then mash the strawberries and put through a strainer. Add the gelatin to the strawberries. Heat the orange juice with the sugar for a few minutes to dissolve the sugar but do not let boil. Add this mixture to the strawberries and gelatin. Measure out all the liquid which should make about 1½ quarts. If not, add enough water to complete. Grease a form with oil of sweet almonds. Place 1 layer of whole fresh strawberries in the bottom of the form, cover with ⅓ of the gelatin and place in the refrigerator until mixture starts to jell. Then place another layer of fresh strawberries on top, cover with more gelatin, chill and repeat. Then let the mixture jell completely. When ready to serve, turn out, cover with crème de chantilly or the cream, whipped with 4 table-spoons sugar and a few drops of vanilla extract. Decorate with whole fresh strawberries.

MANGO JELLY

2 pounds ripe mangoes
2 pounds sugar

WASH the mangoes thoroughly and boil in water with the skins. When tender, peel and put through a fine strainer. Then add in the sugar. Heat over a low flame, stirring constantly, until mixture sticks together. Place in the desired form, chill and serve.

QUINCE MARMALADE

4¼ pounds quince, perfect and without any bruises
6⅓ pounds sugar

Peel the quince, quarter and place in a pot with enough water to cover. Boil and when tender, put through a fine strainer and remove seeds. Make a hard stringy syrup by boiling the sugar in water and then mix in the quince mixture. Continue cooking, stirring constantly until mixture reaches desired consistency.

PUMPKIN AND COCONUT JAM

3¼ pounds of pumpkin
3¼ pounds sugar
1 grated coconut

Peel the pumpkin, boil a few minutes and then put through a strainer. Add in the sugar and heat, stirring constantly. When mixture sticks together, add in the grated coconut and continue cooking and stirring for a few minutes longer. Remove from heat and serve in a compote dish.

COFFEE

S E C T I O N   S E V E N T E E N

••C O F F E E ••

No BRAZILIAN cookbook can be complete without a dissertation on a subject dear to Brazilian hearts —coffee.

Coffee —according to some historians— was being served as a beverage as long ago as the 600's A.D. far away in ancient Araby.

According to a more charming legend, however, the chronic coffee drinker can thank an Abyssinian goat-herder —*Kaldi,* by name— for the availability of his favorite beverage. Kaldi, or so the story goes, was tending his herd as was his wont on the rolling hills of Abyssinia when he noticed that some of his goats seemed to be much peppier and much happier after eating berries from the *kaffia* shrub. (The confirmed coffee drinker can well understand the reactions of Kaldi's kaffia-berry eating goats —he feels much the same way after his first morning cup of coffee.) In any case, Kaldi reasoned, what's good for the goats is good for the master —and so he tried the berries— with happy results. From such humble beginnings, mighty enterprises grow.

The Arabians tried to keep the origin of their stimulating dark brown beverage a "trade secret" so as to maintain a monopoly on coffee, but Kaldi appears to have been less secretive about his "find." The magically stimulating bean found its way to Turkey where the enterprising Turkish merchants soon made trading in coffee a profitable business. From there, coffee quickly spread to the other oriental and mid eastern countries and, in 1588, coffee made its first appearance in Europe —brought to Venice by the Venetian traders returning from Turkey.

The coffee drinking fashion soon became the rage in all of Europe. In Sweden, in fact, coffee drinking became such a national "addiction" that the government tried to forbid its consumption. The Swedes went through a period of coffee "prohibition" and bootlegging until the government admitted defeat and legally allowed the Swedes to do what they had continued to do all along. According to statistics, the Swedes, today, are the greatest coffee drinkers (per capita) in the world.

The Dutch found that coffee and spices went hand in hand. They planted the Arabian coffee plant in their spice-rich colonies of Java and Sumatra which became among the world's greatest coffee-producing areas. Later they expanded their coffee operations to the New World —to Surinam (Dutch Guiana).

The French next became interested in the cultivation of the now world-famous coffee plant. Some say that a French officer brought the coffee seedlings from Europe to the New World, sharing his drinking water with them so that they could survive the long ocean journey. Others claim that the seedlings were spirited out of Surinam into neighboring French Guiana. In any case, the French became coffee growers and, like all the rest, tried to keep the operation a secret so as to establish a monopoly on coffee production. Like all the rest, they failed. An enterprising Brazilian officer, Sergeant-Major Francisco de Melo Palheta, paid a visit to French Guiana and, on his return to his native country, smuggled some of the precious coffee seeds out of the French colony into Brazil.

It was a long meandering journey, from the Arabian peninsula to this lush tropical country, but it was worth it, for it was in Brazil where the coffee plant found its true home.

The Brazilian climate and habitat smiled on Palheta's handful of coffee seeds —and Brazil's coffee empire flourished. Though they made no secret of their coffee operations, Brazilians soon had a virtual monopoly on coffee production. Today it is, uncontested, the world's largest coffee producer.

In the United States —where, after the Boston Tea Party, coffee became the patriotic brew and the time-honored "coffee break" is today as traditional as the Fourth of July— Americans drink coffee to the tune of approximately 270,000,000 cups per day. The United States, in fact, is the world's largest coffee consumer (averaging about two-thirds of the world's annual supply). And Brazil is the one chiefly responsible for quenching this unsatiable "coffee-thirst" of their North American neighbor —approximately half of every cup of coffee drunk by an American is supplied by the Brazilian coffee industry. The United States Department of Agriculture, furthermore, recently announced that all coffee mixtures should contain Brazilian coffee to ensure flavor and quality.

As coffee production made its way from the East to the West, from the Ancient to the New World, the ways of the coffee drinker changed, too. The Arabians drank their brew bitter and with the grounds. The Turks began to add spices to their aromatic beverage.

It took the sweet-toothed Europeans to add sugar to their coffee —at a time when sugar was a commodity only available in an apothecary shop! (From that time, the sugar industry and the coffee industry went hand in hand.) In England, sugar candy — and occasionally even mustard— found its way into the coffee cup. In Holland, the Dutch sweetened theirs with honey and spiced it with cloves, cinnamon and cardamon seeds. Then, finally, the Dutch Ambassador to China tried imitating the Chinese with their tea and added milk to his coffee, a custom which stuck. The Viennese added whipped cream, the French laced it with liquers and Frederick the Great is said to have brewed his with champagne.

The Brazilians, of course, don't believe in such tomfoolery. With them, coffee drinking —like coffee producing— is an art to be cultivated and respected. No Brazilian meal is complete without *"cafézinho"* —a demi-tasse so potent by American standards that some swear it's strong enough to bend the teaspoon. Occasionally, —usually at breakfast time— Brazilians will drink *café com leite* —coffee with milk (a misnomer since it is really more milk with coffee: a cup of hot milk flavored with strong, black coffee). Or else, they may ask for *media* —half milk, half coffee. Most of the time, though, they'll ask for *cafézinho* —and stay to discuss politics. It's good for the digestion, they maintain —but it's best for stimulating conversation.

Most Americans, of course, simply say "sugar and cream, please" —but they say it quite often. And that's why there *has* to be "an awful lot of coffee in Brazil."

Regardless of tastes there are...

EIGHT UNIVERSAL RULES FOR MAKING A GOOD CUP OF COFFEE

1. It is absolutely essential that the coffee-making vessel be thoroughly clean. It should be washed thoroughly with hot water *before and after* using.

2. Coffee freshness is important. If bought already roasted in cans or packages, coffee should be used within a week after opening.

3. Using fresh, *cold* water is an important element contributing to the final delightful flavor.

4. To get the best results, use the full capacity of the coffee maker. *Never brew* less than three-quarters of the capacity of the container.

5. Experiment with brewing time until your taste is satisfied. Consistent use of proper timing makes each pot of coffee brewed a pleasing beverage.

6. Never allow coffee to boil. When coffee is boiled, an undesirable flavor change takes place.

7. Freshly brewed coffee tastes best. Coffee should be served as soon as possible after brewing.

8. To make the most tasty cup of coffee, two level measuring tablespoons of coffee should be used for six ounces of fresh cold water. Then, to make regular-strength coffee, use any of the following methods you prefer.

Vacuum Method

1. Measure fresh cold water into lower bowl. Place on heat.
2. Place filter in upper bowl. Add measured amount of "Fine Grind" or "Drip Grind" coffee.
3. When water boils, reduce heat or turn off electricity. Then insert upper bowl into lower bowl. Twist to insure a tight seal.
4. Let most of water rise into upper bowl. Stir water and coffee thoroughly. Remove from heat. Coffee and water should remain in upper bowl no more than 3 minutes.
5. When brew returns to lower bowl, remove upper bowl and coffee is ready to be served.
6. If a cloth filter is used it should be thoroughly rinsed after each use (no soap), and kept immersed in cold water until used again.

Drip Method

1. Preheat pot by rinsing with hot water.
2. Measure "Drip Grind" coffee into filter section.
3. Measure fresh boiling water into upper container and cover.
4. When dripping is completed, remove upper section. *Stir brew* to mix before serving.

Percolator Method

1. Measure fresh cold water into percolator. Place on heat until water boils. Remove from heat.
2. Measure "Regular Grind" coffee into basket.
3. Insert basket into percolator, cover, return to heat, percolate slowly 6 to 8 minutes.
4. Remove coffee basket and serve.

Extra-strength Method

Make extra-strength coffee by using ½ measuring cup of water for 2 level tablespoons of coffee.

Coffee in quantity

ONE pound of coffee serves forty people when combined with from six to eight quarts of water. Place medium grind coffee in a cheese cloth bag allowing room for its expansion since it will double in bulk. This bag should be dropped into the proper amount of boiling water and let stand from seven to ten minutes. Remove the bag, cover the kettle tightly, keep hot, and serve as soon as possible.

HOT CAFÉ BROULOT

Peel of ½ orange, broken into 5 to 6 pieces
2 sticks cinnamon, 4 inches long, broken into bits
10 cloves
1½ demi-tasse coffee cups full of Cognac
7 lumps loaf sugar
5 demi-tasse cups hot, strong black coffee

PLACE first five ingredients into a metal punch bowl. Fill one tablespoon with Cognac. Hold lighted match underneath the spoon, and ignite contents of bowl with the burning Cognac. After burning for about two minutes, stirring constantly with a ladle, pour in slowly from coffee pot, 5 demi-tasse cups hot, strong, black coffee. Ladle at once from bowl to cups. Makes 6 demi-tasse cups of café broulot.

241

ICED COFFEE DRINKS

To make really good iced coffee, always start with good *hot* coffee. Then, use any of the following methods:

Coffee Ice Cube Method

Freeze regular-strength coffee into ice cubes. Pour regular-strength hot coffee over the coffee ice cubes.

Pre-cooled Method

Make regular-strength coffee and cool in a non-metalic container for not more than three hours. It may be chilled in refrigerator if container is tightly covered. Pour over ice.

FROSTY COFFEE DRINKS

Coffee Mist

Pour extra-strength or espresso coffee into old fashion glasses filled with chipped ice. Serve with a long curl of fresh lemon peel.

Viennese Velvet

Fill tall glasses with vanilla ice cream, but do not pack it. Pour hot, extra-strength coffee over ice cream. Top with whipped cream. Serve as a drink-dessert.

Coffee Mocha

To serve four, combine 2½ cups extra-strength, cold coffee, 5 tablespoons chocolate syrup and 1 pint soft coffee ice cream in a mixing bowl. Blend with beater until smooth.

Spiced Coffee

To serve four, pour 3 cups hot, extra-strength coffee over 2 cinnamon sticks, 4 cloves and 4 allspice berries. Let stand an hour. Strain and pour into ice filled glasses. Serve with cream and sugar.

COFFEE TROPICALE

Fill electric blender container half full of finely chopped ice. Pour in 1½ cups cool, extra-strength coffee and 1 tablespoon granulated sugar. Blend until thick and foamy. Pour into 4 tall glasses.

FROSTED COFFEE HAWAII

In mixing bowl, use rotary beater to combine 2 cups cold, extra-strength coffee, 1 cup chilled pineapple juice and 1 pint soft coffee ice cream. Pour into 4 glasses.

COFFEE CUSTARD

3 tablespoons ground coffee
2 cups very hot milk
3 eggs, beaten slightly
4 tablespoons sugar
¼ teaspoon vanilla

POUR milk over coffee, let steep ten minutes and strain. Stir eggs with sugar and add the rest. Mix and strain into small cups. Place cups into shallow pan. Put boiling hot water into the pan until it reaches half way up to the cups. Place in a moderate oven and cook until custard is firm. Serve warm or ice cold.

COFFEE CREAM

2 cups strong boiling coffee
2 tablespoons gelatin
¼ cup cold water
1 cup sugar
½ teaspoon vanilla
1 pint cream

SOAK gelatin in cold water five minutes. Add coffee and sugar. Stir until gelatin is dissolved. Let cool. Just as mixture begins to thicken, fold in one cup of cream stiffy beaten. Place in a mold, first dipped in cold water. Allow to set until firm. Serve cold surrounded with the rest of the cream, whipped. Sprinkle with chopped pecans, blanched almonds, shredded and roasted, or chopped pistachio nuts.

COFFEE CREAM TORTE

8 eggs, separated
½ lb. powdered sugar
½ lb. almonds, grated
1 teaspoon vanilla
2 oz. coffee, pulverized

BEAT yolks until thick. Add sugar and other ingredients, beaten whites last. Bake in two layers in a moderate oven, 350°F.

COFFEE JELLY

2 tablespoons gelatin
1 cup cold water
2½ cups clear, strong coffee
⅔ cup sugar
4 tablespoons lemon juice

SOAK gelatin in the cold water. Dissolve in the 2½ cups of clear strong coffee. Add the sugar, lemon juice and stir well. Pour into wet mold, chill and serve with whipped cream.

APPENDIX

ACARAJÉ: An Afro-Brazilian dish made with navy beans and topped with cold shrimp sauce.

ANGÚ: A type of "mush" usually made by cooking corn meal in boiling water, salted to taste. It may be cooked until it is of a thick (but not firm) consistency, in which case it is usually spooned out hot. It may also be cooked somewhat longer so that, when allowed to cool, it becomes firm and may be sliced and served cold. Angú may also be made with rice or manioc flour or some other farinaceous base.

CAFÉZINHO: Literally, "little coffee": in practice, there is nothing little about it —except the cups in which it is served. Cafézinho is very strong demitasse coffee —potent enough by American standards to "bend the spoon" —and Brazilians drink it morning, noon and night.

CAIPIRA: A simple Brazilian peasant, living in the interior, away from populated areas. The Brazilian equivalent of our "hillbilly."

CAIPIRINHA: An alcoholic drink made with cachaça (a type of Brazilian rum); limes or lemons and sugar. It originated in the Brazilian "back hills" among the Brazilian "hillbillies." When cachaça is not available, some other rum may be substituted.

CARIOCA: A person, dish or anything, for that matter, from Rio de Janeiro, the old capital of Brazil.

CARURÚ: A dish which came to Brazil by way of the Sudan in Africa. The principal ingredients are shrimp, okra and dendê oil, with variations.

CHURRASCO: Barbecued beef —a dish typical of Rio Grande do Sul where are to be found most of Brazil's large cattle herds.

COCONUT MILK: Brazilians extract milk from the coconut by grating the meat and then pressing and straining the resultant milk from it (see recipe on page 173). Usually, ¾ to 1 cup of milk may be extracted from the coconut in this way. In the States, coconut milk may be found in some supermarkets in cans or as dried coconut milk.

CUSCUZ: A type of corn flour pudding, often combined with many different ingredients.

CUSCUZEIRO: A type of pot, somewhat similar to a "Dutch oven," in which the Brazilian housewife cooks her cuscuz dishes.

EFÓ: Another Afro-Brazilian dish, this time made with shrimp and spinach.

EMPADA: A tiny pie or tartlet, baked in a muffin tin or similar baking form which has been lined with pie dough and then filled with meat, chicken, shrimp, hearts of palm, cheese filling, etc.

ESTANCIA: A Brazilian cattle ranch.

FARINHA: The flour made from the manioc plant which, in other sections of the world, also goes under the name of mandioc, manihot, cassava, yuca, etc. American-Portuguese groceries will almost always have farinha or manioc flour, but when this is not readily available, the farina usually found in supermarkets makes a good substitute.

FAROFA: Toasted manioc flour (see *farinha*) —a constant dinner companion in most Brazilian homes. Brazilians often combine the *farinha* with many different ingredients which usually have first been sautéed. In any case, the farofa usually winds up mixed in with whatever is on the dinner plate.

FEIJAO: Beans —all kinds. Brazil is the world's largest producer.

FEIJOADA: A dish which, probably more than any other, means "Brazilian cooking" to the foreigner. It consists of black beans and a large variety of meats and sausages.

FRITADA: A Brazilian dish in which the principal ingredients have been chopped or minced, mixed with beaten eggs and then baked until golden brown. The ingredients may include such things as pieces of ham, bacon, fish, shrimp, potatoes, vegetables, etc., seasoned to taste. Fritada, in short, is a glorified —but delicious— deep-dish omelette.

GAÚCHO: A Brazilian cowboy.

HEARTS OF PALM: "Palmito," as it is also called in Brazil, is the tender terminal bud of the palm tree before it shoots out of the stem. *Palmito* is now being canned and exported from Brazil and is available in some of the larger food markets and shops specializing in imported delicacies. However, when not available, use artichokes or asparagus.

MANIOC FLOUR: The flour made from the manioc plant, also known by the name of mandioc, manihot, cassava, yuca, etc. Where manioc flour is not available, ordinary farina may be used instead. (See also *farinha* and *farofa* above.)

MUQUECA: A typical dish from Northeastern Brazil with fish and oil as the principal ingredients. The fish is generally stewed or simmered with the condiments (or other ingredients desired) and the oil is added at the end for taste.

PAMPAS: The vast grazing lands or prairies of Brazil (also Argentina).

PIRAO: A common Brazilian side dish. It is a type of "mush" made with manioc flour and the liquid from any dish —as for example, fish, shrimp, chicken, or meat dishes— giving off a broth or gravy.

QUENTAO: The Brazilian equivalent of our hot toddy. It is made by heating rum mixed with spices, lemon and sugar.

SARAPATEL: A type of thick sauce or stew made with the coagulated blood, organs and meat of an animal such as pig, turtle or duck, etc.

TUCUPÍ SAUCE: Sauce made from the root of the manioc plant. This is the one recipe which you may not be able to make because its principal ingredient —the manioc root— is not easy to find. However, no Brazilian cookbook should be without this recipe and for that reason alone, it has been included in this one. Until the manioc root is available, use your favorite sauce instead —and hope in the future.

TUTÚ: A dish made with cooked beans (usually black and usually "leftovers") which have been puréed or liquefied and then re-cooked with manioc flour and other ingredients (as desired) to form a firm, but not hard, mass.

VATAPÁ: Another one of those delicious dishes which came to Brazil by way of Africa. Its main ingredients are shrimp or fish, (occasionally fowl), coconut milk, dendê oil and some kind of flour.